5.95/0

D0345430

The Time of Your Life

MYRON C. & MARY BEN MADDEN

THE TIME OF YOUR LIFE

Broadman Press/Nashville, Tennessee

4254-17
ISBN: 0-8054-5417-9

Subject heading: MIDDLE AGE
Dewey Decimal Classification: 155.6
Library of Congress Catalog Card Number: 76-24059
Printed in the United States of America

DEDICATED TO

Our Children:
Mike, Julie, John, Merritt, Ben
Their Spouses:
Joanna, Bill, Linda
Our Grandchildren:
Golden-haired Sara,
Red-headed Gray,
Brown-haired William Myron

Midway life's journey I was made aware that I strayed into a dark forest, And the right path appeared not anywhere.

We climbed, he first, I following, till to sight Appeared those things of beauty that heaven wears Glimpsed through a rounded opening, faintly bright; Thence issuing, we beheld again the stars.

DANTE . . . *the Inferno*

Introduction

One of the good things that is happening in our marriage is that Myron and I are working at communicating better with each other. We are learning to act and react in our present love, understanding, and needs. Ernest Becker, 1974 Pulitzer Prize winner, said, "It takes twenty years of marriage to finally communicate with one's spouse." [1] Our marriage affirms this. This manuscript is evidence of mutual adventure in continuing our search for growth, working together, directing our energy toward the same interests. We risk making public our private experiences for we know they are not completely unique to us. Our personal feelings from them recall laughs and tears but our identification with others has affirmed our common bond with our generation. This bond frees us from separateness. We write this knowing that our knowledge is joint knowledge; our relationship is our special interacting of culture, heritage, society.

Our aim is that Myron share his insight from years of counseling. His presence of tender discernment and humor enables the questions of pain, death, joy, living to be shared at the deep level of common humanity.

My input is from our personal adventure. In some instances I discuss taking information from outside and claiming it to look forward for growth and understanding.

We want to thank Broadman Press for challenging Myron to work on a manuscript addressed to the period of the "middle years"—defined as the age from forty to sixty—give or take a year or so. Since Myron had already committed himself to a full schedule, he accepted the task on condition that I would help. My contribution has been mainly to research our material, make suggestions where illustrations were needed for clarity, and work with our manuscript in the attempt to make it flow.

I found that there was much material about childhood and old age, but the middle years is a period that has not claimed much attention in the past. Our best source of information has been our own experiences.

We gratefully acknowledge Carole Pearce's contribution to this endeavor. She typed the manuscript.

We write this with the hope that you will find an identifying idiom.

MARY BEN

Contents

SECTION IV   MATE—CHECKMATE

SECTION V   THE TIME OF YOUR LIFE

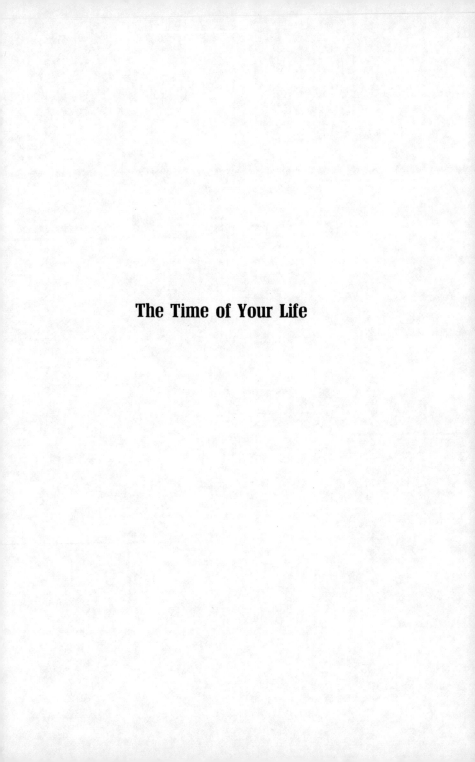

The Time of Your Life

SECTION I
TOWARD FREEDOM AND RESPONSIBILITY

1. Claim Your Power

Midway in life's journey there are many ways we can become lost in the forest and have trouble finding our bearings. I call on you to claim your own power as a person and not squander your resources; you don't have power to waste at middle age, so it's important to get things in focus, get out of the woods, and get on with life.

An Example of Making a Claim

A middle-aged woman whom I knew well was recovering from surgery when I went to visit her. She had just undergone the grief over losing her husband by divorce. She had suffered from some depression for several years in the late stages of her failing marriage.

So it seemed time for me to issue a challenge to see if she wanted to take charge of her own life and be responsible for it. I asked her if she made a claim on life what would she claim. She asked me to spell out what I meant. I said that the good things of life were sitting in jars on a shelf before her and asked her if she would name her jar and claim it.

She immediately answered that she wanted happiness. As we talked she realized that she had made her husband responsible for her happiness, and as a result she had become more and more miserable. The flash of insight that hit her was the truth that if she were ever going to be happy, then *she* would have to find it. She was on the verge of passing the responsibility over to one of her children.

When she got home, she wrote me a note saying, "I'm thankful for my jar of happiness!"

The above woman had given her power away when she put her happiness in the care of someone else. No matter how much you love a person, you don't help them or yourself if you give them such power over you.

In this chapter I ask you questions about your power and also ask you to consider making your claim for your jar on the shelf. There are dozens of ways you can let your power go to others—to authorities, to those who wear the badges of power, of wealth, of influence, or of wisdom.

Giving Power Away and Getting It Back

In my own life I can laugh at how much authority I, as a middle-aged American, gave to the psychology of determinism—we were victims of our preschool years! The behavioral scientists scored our tests, interpreted our dreams, related tics, stammers, unacceptable behavior to our parents. But I cry, too, over the fact that for such a long while I was caught up in its grasp. That was the best information we had. We believed that completeness and wellness were gained by getting one skeleton at a time from the closet to which the psychologist held the key.

I have declared myself free from the determinism of the Freudians, even though I owe Freud a great debt in self-understanding. In fairness to the psychologist, I don't think he wants power over me, but in my own weakness I turned the power over. The doctor, the psychologist, or the "authority" person can help you toward your goal of personal freedom *only if you stay in charge;* otherwise the game is lost.

Freedom is power, but it is also a declaration, not a psychological work. I could not *work* my way out of the bondage to the skeletons of the past; I had to decide to let them be, so I could be. I am not their servant any longer, and I want to claim that you have the right to declare yourself free. You have the power of choice . . . a power the determinist says you don't have, a power B. F. Skinner thinks you shouldn't have, and a power the extreme Calvinists declared you never had.

We are now hearing other psychological voices calling us at middle age to be good to ourselves, to nurture ourselves, or to reparent ourselves. All this may be very good and proper for us. Yet some of us may hear these voices as reversals of the values we have built upon. We have been taught, more or less, to "do for others," "deny yourself," "turn the other cheek," and "go the second mile." All the new voices could sound like: "You were really duped the first half of your life in trying to do for everybody else—now try selfishness for a change." I am not suggesting we do about-face on the values of the past.

I am suggesting that middle age can be a time to turn some things around; it can be a time of looking over our equipment to see whether our vessels are seaworthy for the remainder of our voyage. We might want to check the charts to see if we are on course; we may choose to make a mid-course decision to go in a different direction. It is a self-affirming act to be captain of our own craft or to be in charge of the direction of our life. It is not selfish to claim your own power. I'm not speaking primarily of politics, where you become a kind of power broker, taking some here and giving some there; and I am not despising the political aspects of power. Neither am I encouraging you simply to be a spiritual Robin Hood: taking happiness where it is in abundance and scattering it among the miserable.

Middle age is a worthy time to reconsider what you might have been doing with your power the first half of your life, and it is time to decide if that is the way you want things to be the rest of your life. You are not powerless about what you will do.

What Is Power?

It is not genuine power when you take or seize power from others, such as the power another gives you if you belittle them, put them down some way, or threaten them. Neither do you have much power if you delegate yours to somebody else to use for you, nor if you allow them to take it by threat or some influence they have over you.

To be sure, there are many power games people play. The strong look for the support of the weak in order to grow stronger. They operate on the promise to make the weak more secure if the weak will give up rights to what little they have. On the opposite side, the weak look for a "friendly" strong power to protect them against unfriendly ones. So the "lion and the lamb lie down together," even if the lamb is often on the inside. Suspicion and distrust enter next between the strong and the weak: the strong distrust the weak to stay loyal in what they have committed, and the weak fear the strong will use them instead of helping them.

These power games are played in social life, financial circles, the corporation, organized labor, the institutional church, and in politics. The question comes, what will you do? How will the strong survive without the weak and vice versa? It may be time to get out of the games and play it straight. In the power game, you are never more than a half person, no matter which side you are on. Abraham Lincoln once said, "As I would not be a slave, so I would not be a master." Only a "person" has genuine power. The masters are slaves to the slaves, and the slaves are only the servants of the masters. There can only come the bad feelings that follow the game of using others or being used by others.

At middle age it may be time to make a redecision to get in control of your single unit of power . . . your own person.

The social order has a price it offers for you not to be fully a person. Yet, if you claim the right to be a self, different from every other self on the scene, that difference will become a problem to others. They will get together and try to buy out your interests in going down the path that is single . . . your path. It is your own business if you don't want to be that "single one," but I hold it up to you as your choice, and the path to your power.

A Focus on Direction

Middle age is often a time of decision about the direction of the rest of your life. You can become neutral and just let life happen to you. You can be like a jet plane that climbs half the time between Atlanta and Washington, but at midpoint in the journey turns and begins its descent. We may be imprinted with the belief that it's all downhill in life after we reach the halfway mark. It doesn't have to be that way; you can keep on growing and learning and relating if you choose to do so.

We think of middle age as a time of declining powers. There aren't many baseball, basketball, or hockey players above forty, and George Blanda was one of a kind in football. We don't try out for the Olympics in the fourth decade. Yet, what percent of the population makes its living playing professional sports? We are not out of the game of life because we have no chance at being a quarterback for the Rams or a pitcher for the Cardinals!

Maybe your power as a person needs to be refocused and claimed with positive regard for who you are. Some of your power is in *what you do* but most of it is in *who you are*. So much energy is spent in our younger years trying to become a person like the ones we idolize and model after. It is a sad story in art of how many good artists spent their lives copying the great masterpieces. This seems like a choice to limit one's own creative powers.

No matter what field of endeavor we consider, there is nearly always someone who can do it better than we can. Our task need not be that of beating the masters or even that of copying them. But our power resides in being ourselves in what we are and what we do. Most of us at forty or over are ready to cast off the slavery of modeling our idols and are now ready to settle down to claim who we are.

How We Lose Power

We all suffer from power leaks like an engine that loses compression. We middle-agers tend to lose most power to our children or to our parents, and that comes when we are not careful to define the boundaries. How powerless we feel when a child makes a big claim on us at the same time a parent makes a claim! Either we allow others to take our power away or we unwittingly give it away. In either case we may deplete ourselves without enriching anyone else.

A young woman dreaded the daily call from her grandmother because the grandmother made heavy claims on her. These claims aroused guilt in the granddaughter because she had been cared for very tenderly and lovingly by the grandmother through most of her childhood years. Now it seemed the grandmother was not able to turn loose, and this amounted to a kind of panic for the granddaughter, who had not realized that she could be in control of what she could or would give to her grandmother.

We lose power to others when we hand all the strings over to them to pull at will. An easy setup comes where someone has done a lot in the past to make us feel obligated. Our guilt is also hooked where we have hurt someone in the childhood years, and they flash their scars at us as a reminder that we owe them something. There is the brother with a limp because you let the ladder slip; the sister with a squint because she hurt her eye in a scuffle with you.

Others take our power by threatening us, making us afraid to claim it, or they ridicule us, making us defensive about who we are. We lose power every time we take a put-down from others; this amounts to putting ourselves down. *Our power is drained off because we allow it.*

Our parents originally gave us the power to be by bringing us into the world. Our parents gave us the structure, the house, but they cannot fill it for us—they cannot give it quality. The quality comes in an act of choice that claims what is given. I can spend my years wishing I had a better "house," a different one, a larger one, or one situated in the big city or on the beach.

I develop a power leak in wishing things had been

different. Life can be wished away in yearning for more talent, more intelligence, three more inches of height or black hair. The wishes tend to be endless about how I would have gotten a better start in life, *if* there hadn't been a depression, *if* my father had been more enterprising, *if* I hadn't been born in the smallest village in the county, and on and on.

We lose power to the wish if we return to the past in trying to make that past better, or if we try to correct it in any way. Some things are fixed and do not change, indeed cannot be changed. The past is tops on that list. I am the child of my parents. For much of my younger years I was embarrassed by them. They are dead now, and I would like to have the opportunity to claim them in love without embarrassment, but that cannot be changed. I was not stable enough in my own identity to reach out to them and warmly claim the relationship. Yet since I cannot change all of that now, as much as I would like, I must let it be. What could I do if I decided to work on correcting the regrets of the past? I could use up all my resources at hand in order to accomplish very little, if anything at all.

Claiming What Is

A woman of forty-three expressed her regret that she was not able to put things right for her father. He had retired early for health reasons, and he expected his daughter to make his life happy by giving him care and listening to his needs and woes. After a visit with him she always felt wrung out and empty. He expected what she could not deliver to him, his happiness.

When asked to consider what would happen if she could give her father the happiness he sought from her, she suddenly realized that he would then reach out to her continually. It also struck her that if she could give him what it took to put things right, then her father would tell his friends in the same predicament, and she would feel obligated to respond to their calls to put things right. The more she thought about it, the more she realized that she had been wishing for a power to help that might, in the end, wipe her out because of the demands others would put on her. Instead of bemoaning her inability to help her father, she began to be grateful for things *just as they were*. She could think of doing loving things for her father without the full responsibility for making him happy.

As she reflected on what would make her father happy, she realized he based his happiness on having his health back, his time back, his opportunities back, his youthful years back. She also realized she could destroy her own happiness trying to bring her father the things no man ever got in any generation since the start of life on this planet. She took her own power back when she realized that it was unrealistic to deal with trying to give her father this big pack of impossible miracles. She was glad over the discovery that what she had in her grasp was much greater than what she had been wishing she had. What she did have left her a chance to be free; what she sought would have bound her to her father in such a way that she could never have cut the strings. The more she would have given, the more he would have expected, or the more she would have demanded of herself.

In accepting what *is* as our gift, we are free from the regrets of what might have been, or fears of what might be in the future. Yet acceptance of what is could be a kind of despairing act: I accept it because there is really nothing else I can do or be.

The act of power is claiming what is, choosing it as my very own, while surrendering all the false and unreal options. My chance and your chance to grow comes in owning what is. Suppose, for instance, that the present is very painful because a grief is upon you; you lost someone you loved, you failed to get the job you trained for, you were passed over for the promotion you expected. Whatever the pain or frustration, it is a teacher and an instructor for growth. It is not something you willed for yourself, in fact, you would never invite all that pain. But now that it is given to you, what will you do with it?

Of course you are not thankful for it; if you said at first that you were, you would be a phony. You try to deny that it happened or you justify yourself where guilt or shame are a part of the picture. After you have done all you can to rid yourself of the pain, it follows you, or it waits for you to deal with it.

To be sure, there are patterns of avoidance or ways of denying, running, drugging, or drinking to keep from claiming what is. But when we refuse to claim the pain, we make a choice of sorts to stop growing. The pain will remain until we own it, claim it, and possess it. And even this is only the start: the pain will hurt until we build our inner defenses in the way the body deals with a cut or a burn.

The difference between a wound to the body and a wound to the spirit is that a person can delay the healing of the spirit by denial. For example, a man loses a hand in an accident. His body goes to work and repairs the wound in a few weeks. His mind may also go to work to deal with the pain of the loss to the body image and function—or that man may avoid facing the facts. In the latter case he can drag his grief over the span of a lifetime.

In avoiding what *is* on the side of pain, we carry the unhealed bruises to our spirits from one injury to another. If our bodies had as many open wounds as our spirits, we might be a ghastly sight.

A Time for Healing

Adolescence and youth is a "time for wounding"; the time when we are in the mad dash to do things, to get an education, to have a family, to learn a trade or profession. In the haste of it all, we tend to let the injuries pile up. For example, we don't want to take time out for physical healing such as a broken leg or arm. When the doctor says, "Six weeks in a cast," it sounds like forever. In a similar manner, we store up pain and grief with a promise that we will deal with these when there is more time.

Middle age can be a time when we catch up on the healing: when we let life be what it is; when we stop running, or being loaded with anxiety; when we accept the past for all it says and the present for whatever it is. It can be a time when the feverish pitch abates, and the pulse of the spirit more nearly matches that of the body.

The healing of the person seldom takes place on freeways or in jet planes, but rather it takes place in our being still and waiting. Healing has its own tempo and rhythm; if I rush it, I miss it. At middle age we need to get in step with a rhythm inside ourselves; we may be misled into thinking that the discoveries of medicine and science are signs of a new timing of the spirit. Since physical healing is considerably speeded up by antibiotics, we might falsely impute the same powers to the newest tranquilizer to remove the pains of the spirit.

We are not implying that tranquilizers are bad in themselves. They are meant to help us manage our inner pains until we can have the resources to deal with them. We are misled when we think that medication solves the problem; we sometimes keep the problem and find that the medicine adds another, especially if we come to depend on it.

You will be the one to say whether you come to middle life with unhealed wounds in your spirit. Only you can say whether there are unshed tears held for someone you loved, whether your pride still smarts from somebody's rejection, whether you admitted defeat when it came: an unjust judgment in the courts, an untimely accident, or an unfavorable ruling of the zoning commission.

Before you can fully claim your power, you will need to know if some of it is being lost in proving something. This is related to the past where pains are unresolved. Maybe I have to say that stings to my pride don't hurt, that those who rejected me just weren't worthy of my love anyway; so, I become a modern Stoic in ignoring the pain of it all. I may seem to forget what the hurt was, while most of my energies are spent in keeping it from happening again. When this happens, my strength is used up in defending myself against the return of past pain in some future event.

We live at half strength when we are determined not to allow a repeat of past hurt. Much of the past does come again, and the hurts may repeat: it speaks of growth and maturity when we are able to say we took the full fury of one hurricane, so we believe we can take the winds of the next one. If we learn and grow from adversity, we stop looking for guarantees against the storms; and we build better emotional houses and levees, without squandering all we have on defense.

Claim Your Limitations

As a person you are a mixture of strengths and weaknesses, of powers and limitations. If the weaknesses are denied, you are more vulnerable than when they are accepted. It is human to have weaknesses and limitations—it is also human to want to be rid of them. Yet we can lose our effectiveness as human beings in trying to achieve some sort of superhuman defense against our weaknesses. It is more human to find peace with our limitations than it is to deny them.

The limitations can cover the whole spectrum of existence, all the way from the physical to the mental and emotional. In a rather harsh way a physical handicap can tell you that a career in sports is a closed issue, or a string of *D*'s on your transcript should tell you that a Ph.D. in mathematics is out of your reach. While the romanticism of youth wants to shout protests against every door that closes, the ripeness of middle age can give an OK to those doors. It knows that one good open door may be enough.

Maturity not only accepts a lot of closed doors, it goes further and decides to close a few. The mature person is able to hear life say no, but it is often heard with grief because that no might tell me I cannot do what I most wanted to do. Of course one option is that a person can quit, resign, stop, and live in self-pity and blame. Another option is that one can pick up the pieces and create with them, using what is available for real growth toward new opportunity. For example, we knew a surgeon who lost his right arm in combat. In that experience he lost surgery as his possibility, but he chose to regroup his strength and went on to become a first-rate psychiatrist.

Claim Your Feelings

You are the house where your feelings live. Feelings are "body" things, and the whole range of emotions belong to you from ecstasy to depression and from pain to pleasure. Some emotions may bother you to the point you will not want to claim them, so you deny that you have them. Yet that does not get rid of those feelings. If the census taker should come to take a count of the emotions that live in your house, you do not give him a full count of all who reside with you. You might be more inclined to name peace, joy, happiness, and love, leaving out such characters as hate, envy, greed, lust, and jealousy. Yet the negative feelings are a part of every person; they just may not be paraded in the living room of life.

People tell us what to feel and what not to feel, when to feel and when not to feel. They tell us what is right to feel and what is bad to feel. How often do we hear someone else say, "You ought not to feel that way," or "you have no right to feel like that"? In order to repress the unacceptable, we bring in everything from taboo, custom, logic, reason, ethics, and religion. The miracle of it all is that when someone hears and accepts our bad feelings, those feelings tend to evaporate. At least they take a backseat to the more positive feelings when they are heard by someone who cares. That someone is usually a person who is in touch with the shadow side of himself.

It is a paradox that we often expect to work through bad feelings alone while we expect to share joy, love, gratitude, and all the good feelings with others. This leaves us only half complete in our transactions with others and half done in resolving the bad feelings. There is some psychological law at work that requires us to bring our feelings, both positive and negative, into community and communication if we are going to find meaning, resolution, and growth.

You may need to face the possibility that you feel as you choose to feel. If you are in your bad feelings most of the time, that is your choice. This is not a suggestion that you repress your bad feelings and simply "act" the good ones. If you act like you feel good, you don't really feel good. We are talking about more than "the power of positive thinking." Rather, we are speaking of the power of positive *feelings*, and there is a difference. Before feelings can be positive, the negative ones need to be resolved. For example, depression is a powerful way to control the people around you. You keep them either on edge or in slavish attempts to make you feel better. A refusal to get better leaves them powerless, but struggling. If your depression is chiefly a control device (it can be other things), you can give up the depression when you are willing to give up the control.

Before good feelings can operate freely, you may need "permission" to put away all the heavy stuff that you laid on yourself in childhood or that you allowed others to lay on you. Eric Berne describes the situation of the past that is familiar to us all.

> Negatives are usually said loud and clear, with vigorous enforcement, while positives often fall like raindrops on the stream of life, making little sound and only small ripples. . . . So it turns out that most programming is negative. Every parent fills his children's heads with such restraints. But he also gives them permissions. Prohibitions hamper adaptation to circumstances, while permissions give a free choice.[1]

Berne talks about our need to get on with the permission
of the "blessing" from childhood in order to remove the
"curse." [2] We continue to suffer the curse of bad feelings
as long as we give power to all the past injunctions and
prohibitions. When we claim our own power, we refuse
to allow witchcraft, old wives' tales, and community opinion to dominate our feelings. We can break free from those
"scripts," curses, prophesies, and predictions, and can have
some choice about our own lives and the future we seek.
Certainly we can break the magic spell of a grandfather
who says, "He will never amount to a hill of beans" or
a grandmother who says, "She will never be able to take
care of herself."

We can emancipate ourselves from the ensnarling web
of myth, gossip, and family put-down. Middle age is a
time that we need to start being good parents to our
"child-of-the-past." In the words of Missildine and Galton:

> We can adjust, too, to the fact that we carry within
> us old parental stereotype attitudes we use on our-
> selves and confuse with the truth and that our job
> is to cut through these stereotypes, to recognize them
> for what they are—garbage from the past—and to
> determine that we are not going to use them on our-
> selves any longer but rather that we are going to treat
> ourselves in our own way as we have a right and
> need to do as adults. [3]

Claiming feelings may be a tough challenge; it may even
be frightening. Who knows what demons will stir once
we claim all that belongs to us? We might find ourselves
in touch with the past in frightful ways. Let us also add
that bringing bad feelings to resolution does not imply

that good ones will automatically follow. A life of joy and creativity does not just happen when we've rooted out the kinks, no more than a field grows good crops after we've pulled out the stumps. Crops must be planted and cultivated if we are to get results; so it is with good feelings. We can decide what we want and make our claim with a willingness to be responsible for what we claim.

Other people are not going to give you real power. Indeed they cannot do that, just as they cannot give you happiness. But before you can claim what is you and what is yours, you need to give up what is not you and not yours.

Anything that is not you and not yours, no matter how valuable in the marketplace, is trash for you. It needs to be treated as trash. This enables you to get your values straight and your feelings straight . . . to arrive at what the truth is for you.

Everyone has to deal with some trash. It is ours to recycle and claim; when feelings are straight, thinking is more positive. When we feel good about our life, our power, our family, our friends, we are more positive in living our life—more positive in the thrust to be ourselves. That is where it counts, and it gives us a positive direction.

We need to be in charge of our lives and all the power available as we tackle some of the things that might call forth the best resources we have: namely, our children leaving home and our parents facing the declining years.

Mary Ben will now give the woman's touch, taking a few pages to say how we have struggled, sometimes stumbling, getting lost, or frightened on our way to the middle years. But she does much more—she erases any notion that we are able to stand above and give you "advice" . . . and take away your power.

2. It Was the Summer of '42

Moving into Middle Age

We were born and reared in Louisiana; we married in the summer of '42. Myron's first church took us to the Appalachia region of Virginia. From there he went into the Army as a chaplain. I spent the duration of the war in my parents' home back in Louisiana.

In due course of marriage we found ourselves in the situation described by an Appalachian friend as having "an arm baby, a knee baby, and three yard young'uns." While Dr. Spock's manual was available for reference, my small-town background set the tradition for making my relationship to our children one of relaxed need-demand routine—including breast-feeding and rocking chairs.

In our early forties we began to experience the loss of our parents. My mother was the first to die. I felt a deep shock of loss and grief on losing her. Within a year, Myron's mother died. Contrary to usual life expectancy, both of our fathers outlived our mothers.

I speak of my relationship to Myron, our children, and parents because it was in these basic relationships that I held my identity. My energy went into parenting, home-making, and being a pastor's wife. I felt supported by the security of having parents who loved and enjoyed our

children. Our peer relationships were friends in the fellowship of the church.

At middle age, Myron gave up the pastorate of our
church to become chaplain at the hospital where I was
uninvolved. Our parents were beginning to die. Our older
children were starting to college, leaving home to make
their own lives.

I experienced a real identity crisis.

I found myself asking: Is this all there is for me? What
is this depression I keep feeling? Who am I? What's happening to me? Where do my relationships and obligations
stop, and where do *I* start?

My boundaries had been set by my parents, children,
and church relationships. My questions were vague feelings
that struggled for meaning. My identity need had been
fulfilled in carrying out the role shaped by these relationships. Uncertainty and insecurity filled that vacuum
which the thrust of busyness had filled.

With a Little Help from Our Friends

During this period of introspection that I have described,
I had exaggerated feelings of isolation, loneliness, and
anxiety. A physical checkup showed health about normal
for my age.

I felt frustrated and cheated that Myron helped so many
people work through their problems. Because of loyalty
to him and "our image," I felt that I had no one to confide
in. I do not want to give the impression that Myron and
I did not talk. We have always spent his nonworking hours
together. With a new job, his working days were full and
long. He enjoyed his work and felt a sense of commitment
to the challenge.

When we talked and my feelings came out scared, he

reassured me. When he felt my need for approval, he blessed and affirmed me.

When he experienced my anger, he dodged. Once when our children were small, Myron had a meeting in a nearby town. The children and I went along for a little holiday. The work was in a discussion-type situation. Myron was the resource person. He presented his material. Several persons asked questions and made comments. I volunteered a response. Myron later described my input to a friend. "There Mary Ben sat—saying the very opposite of what I had just been saying—and with such authority!" He has come to describe it as the "often in error, but seldom in doubt" approach to dialogue. Though it was spring, I recall the trip home as a long, cold ride.

During that time quite a number of articles appeared in popular magazines addressed to the subject of the care and nurturing of husbands; how to make your marriage work. One article spoke to me as if Myron were looking over the shoulder of the writer, prompting her. The essence of the article was: one of the worst things that a woman can do is to embarrass or contradict her husband in public! I felt terrible. I knew we had a good marriage, but I was opting for a perfect one. I was really trying hard. While we'd never seen a perfect marriage, somehow I had hoped we might be the ones to make it.

Now I realize that loving concern is not always enough. You sometimes have to have some knowledge and information to interpret what is going on—some insight to understand what is happening inside you. At that point neither of us could draw aside and objectively look at what was going on between us. The energy from my frustration at times made bad feelings for him, for our children, and for me.

Finally I went to my friend who lived next door and told her that I needed someone to talk to. She put me in touch with some concepts that had real meaning for me. She knew my family, affirmed that I loved and cared for our children and their friends. I loved Myron as himself. Therein lies the moral of this tale.

I was holding up an impossible ideal for myself. I was measuring ME against an unrealistic set of expectations. I needed to relax and give myself permission to be a human being in need. For many years, as a pastor's wife, I had talked with young mothers about their problems with children, husbands, parents, and friends. Now I had to learn to receive what I had freely given.

I borrow a verb from Transactional Analysis to identify the meaning that the theological concept of grace gives to me.

Grace means being able to nurture yourself. It means feeling that it's OK to be human. Grace for me is being able to stretch out my hand and heart and receive affirmation.

Do you remember the emphasis in the sixties? "You are acceptable just as you are," "God loves you just as you are." "I love you just as you are." I remember Myron's tease: "I can accept everybody just as they are, except Mary Ben, and I keep hoping she'll change."

About this time he began to participate, as a resource person, in a unique retreat center, Laity Lodge, at Leakey, Texas. I had an opportunity to participate in small conversation groups. My group leader was Bill Cody. I remember my anxiety, my insecurity in anticipating this experience. I knew I would say the wrong thing, give a poor image when I felt I ought to give a good one. Our sharing in group conversations brought affirmation and healing to my spirit. The climate of warmth and freedom created by Bill for the group helped all of us realize it's all right to be human—to share our feelings. This helped me begin to claim my power and worth as a person, and in turn enriched our dialogue as a couple.

SECTION II
THE POWER AND PLACE OF FEELINGS

3. When You Feel Abandoned

When you are alone in your woods, you can despair over being abandoned. This feeling is common at middle age when our children start leaving home and when our parents begin to show age, illness, and death comes. These experiences bring the feeling of loss of power and worth because our primary relationships are giving way on both sides, leaving us exposed, cold, uncovered, unprotected.

I planted two little dogwood trees and was baffled when one of them grew well and the other stalled and seemed stunted. Then along came a hurricane, blowing a pine tree across the small dogwood, which seemed the certain doom of the dwarfed tree. When spring came, the glory came, and the crippled, blighted, injured dogwood took on a spurt of growth and surpassed its mate in one year. My little dogwood spoke to me that year, and it told me that what was being done in nature was also being done in the spirit.

As middle-agers, we are in the middle between two generations, between our children and our parents; at this time the winds blow and bring us to great stress. On the one hand our children are leaving us for their own lives, and our parents are leaving us in another way. They are moving down the slope that leads to loss, loneliness, dependency, illness, and death.

It is not my purpose here to sing a sad and mournful

song, but to affirm that life goes on. Our passing along
this path can be good unless we insist on being exceptions
to the general course and the "shocks that flesh is heir
to." We don't have to wander in abandonment.

The purpose of this chapter and the next is to deal with
some of the meanings of being in the middle of crises
brought on in relation to our children and our parents.

Children Leaving Home

When the first child leaves home, we are hit with the
reality that for this particular child, our home has served
its main purpose. There is the pain of separation, the
anxiety over the child's comfort or ability to cope out there,
the regrets of things not done that we might have done,
and remorse that we did many things we wish we hadn't
done. We hurt over the empty space they leave behind,
but all the while we know that the real hurt is in our
spirits. Our lives had been intermingled and interrelated
in more ways than we realized until we started to cut the
strings. Those "strings" seem to hold the vital juices that
threaten to drain out when we apply cutting edges.

There's no turning back, the separation process has
begun; the purpose we held at the start is now being
accomplished, but why didn't we know how it would hurt?
Or did others tell us and we just didn't hear? Children
leaving home are expressing their own growth needs which
we bless with our thoughts, but often resist in our feelings.

The Need for Idols *Versus* Models

Into the early beginnings of growth, the small child
makes parents into idols. Our then-five-year-old John once
asked, "Daddy, how much difference is there between you
and God?" Adults are so big and powerful and full of

knowledge and wisdom to the child!

Mother performs magic in the kitchen every day, turning mixes into cakes and dough into bread. Dad's omnipotence enables him to take a few tools, lumber, and make a garage! All this ability, strength, and wisdom seem unreachable for the child. The little girl may come out saying, "I'll never be able to cook like my mother." She even may take a vow never to surpass this seeming greatness. The little boy may say, "I will never catch up to my father," and he may resolve never to aspire to such strength and wonder as he witnesses his father using a power saw or a noisy lawn mower. Daddy reinforces the resolve with "Stay away from the saw! Never put your hands or feet near this danger!"

There is such power and splendor that seems to surround the unreachable and immortal world of the adults! Thomas Traherne once expanded on his own childhood vision of his city:

> The men! O what venerable and revered creatures did the aged seem! Immortal Cherubims! And young men glittering and sparkling Angels, and maids, seraphic pieces of life and beauty! Boys and girls tumbling in the street, and playing, were moving jewels. I knew not that they were born or should die. . . . The city seems to stand in Eden. . . .¹

The teenage person experiences shocks in relating to the misjudgment of this earlier Eden. Nature helps through the sudden spurt of growth that sends the girl child to the height of her mother and the little boy stretches out to a gangling, awkward human just as big as his father, often bigger by the time he is fourteen. We come to "the fall" when little people grow up. The fall is not theirs, but their parents' who have fallen from the lofty heights of Mount Olympus . . . we may no longer be gods. To be sure we never were gods, and we never made such claim for ourselves, but we once were such in the eyes of the six-year-old. To be sure the child holds to the myth about us as long as possible, but growth and reality demand that the idols go . . . and with that Eden goes.

It is no easy process for the child to experience a crumbling of that which held his world together . . . the assumption of the unlimited and immortal properties of his parents. This is some of the meaning of Humpty-Dumpty: a world shattered with no way to put it together again. It is also the meaning of Thomas Wolfe's, *You Can't Go Home Again.* It is the words of a young woman who said, "All my gods have died." Shakespeare also speaks the same truth at the death of the great Anthony. "Young boys and girls are level now with men" (*Anthony and Cleopatra,* Act V, Sc. 1).

Most of you will remember the mourning of the entire nation upon the death of President John F. Kennedy. The mighty had fallen, and we all felt again some of the old despair of the teen years when we suddenly realized that parents were not gods but human beings. The same held true of the young president, so powerful three days before, but now, in a flag-bedecked coffin, being helplessly jostled down Pennsylvania Avenue on a caisson. Could not even "this flesh keep in a little life"?

Hawthorne gives us the picture of a beautiful, innocent young woman, Phoebe, who has to deal with the truth and reality about the utter human qualities of persons in high station:

Phoebe went . . . with queries (about) whether judges, clergymen, and other characters of that eminent stamp and respectability, could really, in any single instance, be otherwise than just and upright men. A doubt of this nature has a most disturbing influence, and, if shown to be a fact, comes with fearful and startling effect on minds of the trim, orderly, and limit-loving class, in which we find our little country girl.[2]

So it came to Phoebe to realize that the idols had clay feet, and it comes as well to most teenagers.

The suffering of parents at this point is one of abuse from youngsters who blame and scorn because we couldn't keep reality from coming through to them. Ultimately this is not just a reality that parents are frail, mortal, ordinary humans, but young people must consider their own mortality once they have peeped at it in parents.

Eric Berne speaks of *scripts.* "Each person decides in early childhood how he will live and how he will die, and that plan, which he carries in his head wherever he goes, is called a script." [3] These early scripts, or what otherwise might be called "childhood vows," may be tested against a growing sense of reality, and they may be changed. However, Berne points out: "Scripts are usually based on childhood illusions which may persist throughout a whole lifetime; but in more sensitive, perceptive, and intelligent people these illusions dissolve one by one leading to the various life crises. . . . Among these crises are the adolescent reappraisal of parents." [4]

We parents cannot move ourselves from the position of idols to that of models. The young person must do this

at his or her own pace. As an idol, we are interior to the child's thinking and feeling; as a model, we are moved out of the interior space and put in an exterior relation. The young person will decide whether he is able to take the idol and reshape it into a model. He may reject us totally and move to others for his models, and that is OK, but it hurts!

The Need for Distance *Versus* Intimacy

The young tree doesn't grow well under the shade of the parent plant, and the same holds true for the human offspring. There needs to be distance, space or room for growth and expansion, for stretching and maturing without too much intervention from the parents.

The little child raises few if any questions about closeness and intimacy to parents. The essence of teenage stretching is that of beginning to close doors between the self and the parent. It just might be the need and desire to grow a self that is not totally derived from the parent . . . a self one can call one's own, a self that is apart from what was given by nature and inheritance . . . perhaps a self that is not owned by anyone else, but rather one that is able to stand alone and be in charge of one's own space.

Parents so often see the teenager through earlier experiences where there was an uninterrupted closeness and intimacy, where there was no shame in sharing feelings, plans, hopes, thoughts, and dreams. The intimate details in the relationship seem to bind child to parent and parent to child. Yet nearly every teenage person comes to a definite need to disavow what amounted to earlier childhood vows, made to or before parents. An unthinking parent might ignore the need for distance and try to hold the relationship in the range of where it stood ten years earlier.

Where parents cling to the past, the young person may feel he or she must either regress and hold to early childhood patterns or rebel and throw everything out.

Where the home can relate to this need for growth, the young person is able to salvage what he chooses from the past and add what he chooses for growth and new experience. The need for distance is paramount over the need for intimacy for the young person, at least where parents are concerned. They want to free themselves from too much indebtedness to those who sired, birthed, suckled, handled, coddled, clothed, and fed them. Hence the cry for space and distance.

Young people want to meet intimacy needs with their peers rather than their parents.

This can be a crisis for us . . . the parents. To draw back and let be; to respect the distance that seems so strange to us is a new and different matter.

The Need for Independence *Versus* Dependency

The child in the early years fixes on parents with an unexamined and unthought dependency. The thought of separation brings panic to the child. In her imagination the little girl pictures herself taking over the kitchen from mother and preparing tasty meals for the family, or she can imagine herself as the spotless housekeeper that makes the entire household run smoothly. But an attack of illness to the mother puts that little girl in terror. She is mortified over the very thought of having no mother to meet her actual needs for love and comfort.

The story changes when that same little girl is ready for college or work. She needs home and parents to be available, but not necessary as they once were. It is now that she needs to put to practice some of the fantasies of earlier years as she starts the process of taking care of herself . . . of developing some independence at the very areas that felt comfortably dependent in earlier childhood.

Our little children may feel the contract for their care is forever; these same children later put their inner calculators to work. They soon learn that the childhood image of "forever" is a mistake. The teenagers come to the awareness that parents are mortal human beings with a limited life span. They may even feel that parents would volunteer to travel the entire journey with them and take care of them all their days. But reality shouts down the rhythm of our lullaby to remind them that they need to prepare themselves against the necessary separation that time will thrust upon us all. Parents and children alike need to be able to adjust to the fact that the next generation . . . our children . . . must be able to stand with autonomy and independence when our present props no longer hold.

Growing up and leaving parents is a part of establishing independence. The physical separation from home may come a long while before the young person is psychologically autonomous and independent. We parents might try to handle our pain by using seductions that cripple and bind. Our offers of care may have tempting flavors from the past, or flavors with assurance that our experience can make things safer. If these and other offers fail, we can usually seduce with bank accounts, bikes, cars, credit cards!

The young person fears bad decisions, and she may call Mother to help her decide which dress to buy or wear, what colors are right for her curtains, or she may call on Dad to tell her what to do with a flat tire. These messages usually are saying, "It's lonely out here, and I need to know you are there." The parents might hear the message, "Help me, I'm drowning!" and this is especially true if there are a few tears of frustration in the call for some help.

These requests may afford the chance to teach a few things we know, things we couldn't teach before a crisis or need was present. Yet a takeover at such times will prevent learning and growth.

The young person getting on his or her own needs to practice decision-making regarding a thousand things. These include decisions about living space, transportation, clothing, and the choosing of friends. If parents are hovering over the offspring with ready answers, this can bring on a crisis in which parents either are asked to completely take over or they are told to get out. Needless to say, the needs for growth toward relative self-sufficiency and independence are not served when either of these occur.

When a young person is establishing a stance of some independence, we parents serve growth needs better in "doing with" rather than "doing for."

It may be a sad truth for young persons that, in claiming their own place in growth, they are shutting some doors toward parents. Perhaps these doors don't need to be closed just on one side. Parents must go on living. Their needs may now be put first. It is growth for parents when we can say no to unreasonable demands.

The Need for Freedom *Versus* Control

At the beginning of life, control is mainly physical. The infant has no control over the body and its functions; without the help of parents, the human infant would be the most helpless in all nature. Many early teachings shift the focus from direct physical control to verbal control.

The mother can shout "stop" sooner than she can run to the child and catch his hand before he touches the stove or hot iron, or before he walks into the street. The early injunctions are mostly stoppers in case of harm or inconvenience. More and more controls over the physical life of a child are released in favor of psychological ones. Every parent goes through the range of prohibitions from "stop" to "shut up" and "don't touch it," "dirty," "hot," "nasty" to "shame," "ugly," "bad," and "naughty."

As long as the control in any area is with the parents, the child obeys the injunctions, not for his own sake, but for the sake of giving the parents what they demand. He may not be aware that to "stop" will save his life, but he does know that it makes mother happy if he does . . . furious if he doesn't!

While the mother develops methods of controlling the child, a process is going on with the child whereby he develops countercontrol of the mother. Ernest Becker puts it this way about the child: "He has to keep the feeling that he has absolute power and control, and in order to do that he has to develop independence of some kind, the conviction that he is shaping his own life." [5]

The awakening of the teens is the awareness that the parent has more control over the child than was imagined. The battle that ensues is one of taking over more control of one's existance, of becoming more responsible for one's destiny, of saying no to parents about their control. Yet most of the resentment felt by the offspring is toward his inner fear of passivity and dependence. If these fears keep their clutch, there can be little autonomy and freedom.

Whereas the first separation was physical, symbolized by birth, now there is the need for a new birth of freedom . . a psychological one that begins dissolving the bond that stands between parent and child. This can happen easier where there is a renewed physical separation of moving out of the house (the family's body) into a new space that the teenager can call his own. This is nearly always a move fraught with anxiety and concern because of the newness and dread of a new and unfamiliar (unfamily) surroundings. The anxiety can be a tightness or breathlessness because it is like birth when the child had to wait for breathing to begin. Freedom is a decision, a "leap," a move from the comfortable to the uncertain, from the solid to the unformed, from a mass to a space.

It is a strange paradox that we parents can look back at our own leaps into uncertainty as our growth experiences. And even as we do this, we attempt to build every possible security around our children in order that they will not have to face that kind of risk. To that end we work to have every rock padded, every thorn covered, every bruise doctored, every pain tranquilized, and every risk insured.

The Aging and Death of Parents

Let us move to the other end of the spectrum: the problem of dealing with our parents' getting older and dying. At the same time our children may be taking leave of us for college or work, we feel caught in a crosscurrent of streams flowing in different directions. Our loyalties to children and our loyalties to parents frustrate our energies in giving money, love, and time. Each of us has to work out our answers according to our resources.

Parents: Acceptance *Versus* Rejection

It is no easy matter to accept yourself as you are. There is resistance because it would seem that what you accept, you don't change. But the truth is—in fact—you can only begin to change as you accept *what is!* In the usual approach, we tend to deny the unacceptable within ourselves. We hold this unacceptable within ourselves for very private struggles of reshaping and reordering, believing that the encounter of appearance was real. An honest look at things will make us admit the real person was hidden behind the dress.

Our parents can be a threat to us because they reveal openly what we have struggled privately to keep concealed about ourselves. They represent a tearing of our Sunday garments, an exposure of our repressed fears, or a shouting from the housetop what we had whispered in the ear. This is especially painful where upward social climbing finds us a notch or two above our parents. We don't want our origins to be uncovered in front of our peers. "In the upward climb, it is not sufficient that the climber should affiliate himself with the class level above him, assimilating their culture; he must also break . . . with the class level left behind, most often . . . his parents." [6]

At middle age we may need to examine our climb and our search if it takes us out of reach of our origins, that is, our parents. We cannot be real persons and at the same time deny the roots of our beginnings on the pilgrimage of life. There is a wisdom of rural people that says a boy shouldn't get above his "raisin'." Hence, acceptance of parents as they are can be a step toward maturity and reality. We do not have to abandon our ambitions; our parents very likely would not want that. Their intentions from the start most likely were that of helping us achieve success greater than theirs. Such success may be a false claim if it shuts out the ones who fired our ambitions to begin that climb up the ladder.

Like it or not, our parents are a part of us—their hand-writing on us is much of the script by which we live. The ability to accept our parents as they are is a strong begin-ning along the path of self-acceptance. And acceptance of parents may be making peace with faults we have long disliked. It may be a permission within ourselves to simply stop trying to change them. We should know by the middle years that our attempts to change them are not very fruitful. D. H. Lawrence says of a wife set on changing her husband: "In seeking to make him nobler than he could be, she destroyed him." [7]

Parents as Persons *Versus* Problems

To be sure, our parents have problems; and those prob-lems increase as they face aging, retirement, poor health, lowered income, inflation, and loneliness. What we've said about claiming your power applies to parents. Guilt and obligation are not cords to tie a person down because parents brought us into the world and nurtured us to adulthood. To work from the motivation of such feelings causes us to lose sight of the most important thing that is in the relationship—children and parents can relate to each other as adults—as peers. The harder a person tries to work out problems between parents and children on the basis of what the children owe the parents from the past—the heavier the relationship becomes. Love and un-derstanding have to bridge a gap that cannot be paid for with money and works, but accepting limitations is part of the process.

In dealing with your parents, as in dealing with your children, it is important not to play games with each other. This might call for some adjustment in your behavior patterns, because this means being straight and honest . . .

relating as peer rather taking a greater or lesser position. It might call for breaking traditions about what you have always done for Christmas or birthdays. Old habits can be updated.

It is understandable that your parent or parents may make you the most important person in their lives, but this carries no obligation for you to make them number one on your list. To be sure there once was a time when that was true. But if marriage has any meaning for you, you dropped the contract of firstness with parents when you committed yourself to a mate. Of course they will be hurt when you have to demonstrate that other persons are ahead of them in your considerations. But that is part of the pain of reality. If you try to play games at this point, everybody will get hurt worse in the long run.

Being straight means you share responsibilities honestly with brothers and sisters, letting them know your limitations. These limitations cover financial as well as emotional resources. You never have unlimited reserves in either of these areas.

It is not the burden or responsibility of any of the children to make parents happy. Their happiness and emotional well-being are chiefly their own responsibility. If they are unable to be happy, they could use their unhappiness as a way to control and keep anyone from being happy. Can you accept the fact: if your parents are unhappy it may be their decision to be that way? Are you able to bless their unhappiness?

Parents as Peers *Versus* Super-Humans

The "child" in us can get hooked very easily in relating to our parents. At middle age it is time to psychologically "call no man father." By this I mean it is time to see parents as peers. Of course there was a time when they were gods on Mount Olympus, but that time has passed. They are human beings, and that is OK. It is time to forgive them for failing us, for failing to keep on getting taller as we grew, or getting stronger as we gained in strength.

When people are adults to each other, they are all the same size.

In their aging and growing toward senility, parents seem to be breaking our childhood dreams; dreams that must be broken because mortality and weakness are a real part of the whole human drama. What seemed an unbreakable chain now begins to weaken and falter. Are they letting us down? Will they allow our own reflections about our humanness to break through?

Let me affirm that the realization of our limits is a part of our own growth, not a sign of failure, sin, or wretchedness. Only as we accept our parents where they are and for what they are can we continue a healthy process of claiming our own place in life.

Parents: Nursing Home *Versus* Any Home

When Medicare, Medicaid, and the many extra benefits in federal programs for the aging became available, I felt that our social engineering had come of age. What could be a better move than to see that our old people are well cared for? It seemed this move would even take stress out of middle age, because the message would go back down the years: "You don't have to worry about being cast off with no place to live or with nothing to wear." It seemed the new gains for the aged would free us up against fears of privation.

The very opposite of my hopes has actually been accomplished. To be sure, it is good to have the guarantee of food, clothing, and shelter in the declining years. But this is gained at great expense to persons. It is shocking to realize that these good benefits often come at the loss of civil rights. The civil rights of the old are not well guarded. The benefits come with emphasis on physical care with less attention being given to the emotional and affectional needs.

Let's sum up the picture in the words of Halbert L. Dunn: "Institutionalization, no matter how graciously conceived or tenderly administered, is a form of lifelessness before death. So fellowship for the older person is a must." [8]

The modern nursing home is a product of our social planning. It was likely conceived with the many physical needs in mind, with the assumption that if these were met in a clean, comfortable, medical, and well-lighted place, that this would be sufficient. Who could have imagined the despair that would hover in a place where old people are assembled, shuffled, regimented, and doctored? There is only the other spectacle I have observed where there was more massive despair: Mauthausen, one of the German concentration camps captured by our troops in World War II. We have had a decade of experience with the nursing home. While we condemn ourselves for some failure, we commend ourselves for learning; and we need to face the challenge for improvement and change.

For one thing, we need to make children and old people available to each other—they actually need each other to complete some primitive hungers. They tend to understand one another because children have not yet gotten into the social climb, and the old are already out of it—hence they have a focus on many of the same values, values that are personal and natural. Children have a quest (or question), and old people sometimes have an answer mellowed with thought, or they have patience with those questions that never can be answered.

While my words about nursing homes may sound judgmental, or even cruel, I must say that these homes are meeting a great need. I lend no support to the idea of abolishing them, but rather to changing them.

The retirement homes that are planned by church or community groups seem to be opening the way to some good developments. One advantage seems to come from commitment by those who have a share in planning their future. Another is in the fact that many of the residents know each other. This results in more company, more parties, and a greater sharing.

Another area of need is to cut down on the crowding together of so many old people in one place. We have some expansive stretches of unused or little-used real estate in America. At present not many of our older citizens wake up to the singing of a mockingbird or go to sleep with the wind whistling in the tops of pine trees, the chirping of crickets, or the night call of the whipporwill. To be sure, not all the elderly, especially the ones reared in the city, would prefer a more rural setting. But it would be good to have a choice. You could argue that the modern hospital is too inaccessible to the rural area, or the doctors all concentrate their work in the city, and some of these are valid objections. Can we at least ask questions about how we can solve some of these problems?

One of our failures comes in the area of identification. We tend to push the aging persons out of reach, maybe because we don't want to tie ourselves to the same chain that holds them. Well, we are tied to it, whether we admit it or not. And solving the problem for our parents is solving it for ourselves and our children.

Our case here is not one to settle the matter about where

our aging parents will live. Sometimes we don't have very good options. But if our aim is that of doing what we can to enrich the lives of our parents, we are going in a good direction. It is a proper perspective on the situation to remember that while the physical needs may be numerous, the social, emotional, and affectional needs are really paramount. The fears of the little child about separation from his parents is not first that he will starve or freeze, but that there will be nobody to love him. It is not different for those who are threescore and ten.

A prayer of Kierkegaard might set the mood for what we've been saying:

> Oh, Thou that givest both the beginning and the completion, may Thou early, at the dawn of day, give to the young man the resolution to will one thing. As the day wanes, may Thou give to the old man a renewed remembrance of his first resolution, that the first may be like the last, the last like the first, in possession of a life that has willed only one thing.[9]

Giving Parents Up in Death *Versus* Holding On to Them

When I stood at the coffin of my father, after the funeral service, the "child" in me came to the surface. I looked at his hands folded, and that sight was unbelievable. I remembered those hands when they seemed indestructible and powerful. They had magically untied the knots in my shoelaces when as a little boy I was too sleepy to struggle with the tangle. I had seen him wrench off jar tops and take an egg from boiling water. He would snatch a coal of fire with his naked fingers from the edge of the fireplace and put it in his pipe. Now these hands were folded in surrender with no more power and no more magic. How the mighty had fallen!

The "adult" in me had accepted my father's demise several months before his death. But the "child" in me waited for the last breath and the folded hands. So it may be with you. Death calls for a disengaging, a grieving, an acceptance of this most natural event in our pilgrimage.

There is no way we are supposed to feel in the loss of parents. All I can affirm is that we need to finish our business with the dead, and that is the process of grief.

We cannot, out of a sense of duty, loyalty, or love carry the dead with us. The contract for living calls on us to unmix our lives from those who have died. When we genuinely grieve, we allow that our common existence, once intertwined with the loved one, is springing free that we might invest it anew with those in the land of the living.

Yet the question comes: who will take his place, or who will take her place? The assumption behind that question is that there needs to be a volunteer among us to move into the vacancy. This "place" is often nudged upon one of the living children to carry as an act of loyalty. For example, a man said, "My brothers were so hurt by my father's death that I held up for them, and let them cry, but I never had time to let down. Now I can't get to my tears." Families are unknowingly cruel to the one they anoint to "bear up" and be a support for everyone else; that one becomes a sort of family priest or priestess. (We will deal with this more in the next chapter.)

The Inheritance: Blessing *Versus* Curse

It is a common sight to see the death of a parent bring on much frustration and confusion among the children We witness discord and all manner of struggle after the funeral. The focus of the conflict usually centers around the division of the property or the estate. We can get some light on the problem if we remember that the possessions represent the "blessing" of the parent in a very special way. They are the "remains" and in a selfish desire not to tear this seamless robe, each child may cling to the possessions as a kind of last chance to secure the blessing for himself. Where the grief is not finished, the belongings are a way of denial. Hence, there can be quite a squabble over a watch, a ring, or some special family heirloom.

Where family members can be straight about their feelings, and honest about their memories as well as open about their desires, there is a better chance of untangling things and making settlement. Feelings are going to be hurt, no matter what settlement is made, but if all the feelings are represented, there is a better likelihood that some kind of justice will prevail in the family.

In giving up our parents in death or in allowing our children to leave us, we are doing what we must. People can do what they must. The other choice, that of holding on to what we lose, has a way of leaving us in the dark forest. In making our claim to grow and learn in all of the pain, we are on the course that will help us see the stars again.

4. Finding Your Way Out of Depression and Grief

A statement of faith: *any experience we have to go through can be rewarding.* I am taking the positive approach to the painful experiences of depression and grief. There is a way to grow in these times; indeed, they furnish the greatest growth we know about. But we usually have to work through them before we can know their value.

At all times we have the option of staying in depression or grief if we choose to do so. I would be the last one to push anyone ahead of his or her willingness to move. There are too many would-be helpers who are ready to urge or push. I think they do it for their own sake. They want you to cheer up so they won't have to deal with their own tears. I don't blame them for that; they are also trying to cope, and this seems to be the best they know.

People usually do the best they can with these crises, and the purpose of this chapter is that of thinking about better means of managing our feelings when we hurt.

Depression

Defining the Issue

Not many persons go through middle age without some heavy moods, especially the mood of depression. I don't want to put you down because you fall into these bad feelings; neither is it helpful if you put yourself down.

You may feel at times that it is more than you can do to keep your head up, your work done, your grass cut, your letters written, and your bills paid. You may wish you could sleep for a month and forget all that is going on around you.

You may feel that the joy has gone out of life, the sun is only half bright, the birds go without song, flowers lose their color, food has no taste, and children have no sparkle. You can feel with Hamlet when he said he lost all his mirth, quit taking exercise, "and indeed it goes so heavily with my disposition that this goodly frame, the earth, seems to me a sterile promontory" (Act II, Sc. 2). Or with Abraham Lincoln you can say that your miseries are so heavy that, if they were distributed among the whole human family, there wouldn't be one happy face.

After your attempts to describe depression, about all you can call the feeling is an "it." It is an unwelcome stranger in your house. You never thought that you gave it a place or a welcome, yet it seems to be the best nourished member of the household. It comes when it pleases and takes leave without notice. It reserves the right to trespass upon your time to the point it takes the fun out of your party or it wipes out your vacation. Along with Antonio you say of this heavy sadness:

> But how I caught it, found it, or came by it, What stuff 'tis made of, whereof it is born, I am to learn.
> (*Merchant of Venice,* Act I, Sc. 1)

The essence of depression escapes definition. One day there is a reason for it. The next day the reason is discarded for one that seems better. On through the deep and sleepless nights you try to find a cause big enough to account for so much misery.

You share with a friend the fact that you are down, have lost your bounce, and can't sleep well. She tells you about all your good fortune, your beautiful home, your job, your talents, your children, and concludes that it is bad, wrong, shameful, or even sinful for anyone in your state of affairs to think of feeling that way. *Now, you not only feel bad, but you feel bad about feeling bad!* Your friend has just put a curse on your depression; it is a thing you can't mention to her again. You will have to try harder to be jolly, act happy, and let this "thing" have less sway in your life, especially when you are around her.

The thought strikes you to tell your condition to your medical doctor, yet you are somewhat skeptical after the reaction of your friend. You tell yourself that your doctor may take the same approach. Besides, what right do you have to go to your doctor when the last time you went, he said you were in good health? You need an excuse that will make your doctor take you seriously. The next best thought is to fight this thing until you get a pain or an ache somewhere; that will give your appointment a reason and some respectability. You finally develop a stomachache or a repeated headache; now you have something real, but will you tell him about the gnawing feelings in your spirit, your sleeplessness, your fears that seem so unfounded? You decide to come clean and tell him all.

If you are lucky, your doctor will not treat your stomach or headache as the only problem. After a complete examination, he may give you a tranquilizer to help you sleep. While he may feel the inclination to suggest a psychiatrist, he will likely check your reaction to the idea. He has lost patients by making this kind of referral in the past. He wants to make sure he doesn't so anger you that you go somewhere else for medical treatment.

Not many of us are willing to admit that a part of the cause of depression at middle age is middle age itself. Here are some of the things that get into our minds, thoughts, and feelings:

I'm running out of reasons for my life.

What will I do when the children are all gone?

I never thought my body would slow down!

Why is our marriage under such continual strain?

What will I do if this next job doesn't pan out?

Where will we get the money needed for the hospital costs? Or should I delay a needed operation?

The years are passing swiftly, and mine are more than half gone!

If I could do what I wanted for the rest of my life, what would it be?

With all the push to get ahead, I must now ask, "Who am I?"

These and many other questions go whirling in our heads, and they may not find easy solution.

We've been thinking of things common to both men and women, yet there are things more common to women, others to men.

Women in Middle-Age Depression

Women in middle age are more given to involutional melancholia (though men have it, too). In a woman there are more pronounced body changes, especially in the cessation of menstruation. Along with this goes palpitation, sweating, hot flashes, sometimes weak spells, and dizziness. Since the physical aspects are more dramatic, the influence on the mental life is more direct and pronounced.

A woman is concerned about her attractiveness as a female. She asks if her husband will maintain sexual interest in her as she undergoes the "change of life." It is not uncommon for a woman to become more jealous than usual or a little more suspicious of her mate. She may respond to her own feelings and withdraw, or become more openly demanding of her husband's attention.

In this period, a woman tends more to ignore her mate's need for distance; she may interpret that need as withdrawal on his part and react with rejection and feelings of hurt and injury.

Again the woman is often flooded with feelings she may be unable to sort out, and unless she can sort out the confused feelings, she may react unpredictably, even to herself. When this happens, it follows that communication is strained; it may even be broken.

My own failure with Mary Ben under such circumstances just described came when I tried to interpret what she felt by passing judgment on her feelings, instead of giving her the right to whatever feelings she had, and then coming back to support her feelings. This left her little choice but to put me down about my own feelings.

You see, I never can really tell Mary Ben how she feels. She is the authority there, and the only authority. No one can tell me how I feel since I am the authority in that area. Even to attempt an interpretation of Mary Ben's feelings is about the biggest mistake I can make.

We don't always succeed now, but we try to handle our hassles by one of us being straight about what we are feeling. It nearly always produces a surprise, "I didn't know you felt that way!" It is always a kind of new surprise that Mary Ben can easily accept my real feelings no matter what. But she can't and doesn't accept a feeling I think "sounds" better. I always tend to defend my deeper and real feelings with some sort of rationalization or excuse simply out of habit. But when we don't defend, we usually come out better.

An example might go like this: Mary Ben took my car keys, inadvertently, and was fifty miles away when we talked on the phone. I was in a rage about the keys, I had turned the house upside down, and then I asked her about the keys. Naturally I was ready to put her down. She simply said, after looking through her purse, "I have them—I just blew it." That was all it took to deflate my anger. She took responsibility for blowing it, and there was no more to be said. If she had gone into reasons why it happened, my anger would have gotten worse. There were a dozen things she could have blamed it on, but she didn't pick out a single one of them. Then my mind went to work to justify her, and I could think of all the reasons why she did it, and I justified what she did with no trouble at all.

Men in Middle-Age Depression

Men in middle age are given less to melancholia, and more to "acting out" their feelings of depression. All those questions given earlier get in a man's mind, and he wonders

about his vitality and potency as a male. He may seek
ways to prove himself: this is to say he wants to disprove
that Father Time and Mother Nature are making their
marks upon him.

One of the ways of proving himself is in his work. He
can overload himself with jobs that should be left with
younger men. He may invite more responsibility until he
is caught up in the "Peter-principle," that is, he gets pro-
moted above the level of his ability. The cycle becomes
self-defeating, and he can push himself right into a heart
attack (coronary thrombosis). At any rate the strain of work
and worry will tend to crop out in his body in whatever
system of the body there tends to be a weakness. One
man may suffer damage to his cardiovascular system
(heart), another may be affected in his digestive system
(ulcer or ulcerative colitis), yet another may find stress
in his respiratory system, the lymph system, or perhaps
the genito-urinary system.

Middle age is the time when a man can reap the benefits
of years of experience and wisdom rather than trying to
push the body above its limits. There is an old Arab prov-
erb that says: "The master does more with his eye than
with his hand." So the man of experience is valuable if
he conveys that experience to the young, the ignorant, and
the unskilled.

The threats of change and loss of vitality find some men
acting out their sex fantasies in an affair. They want to
prove that their potency is not diminished, and they may
seek the stimulation of a younger woman. Sam Keen illustrates with his own story what we are saying:

I was approaching the mythical year forty . . .
I left my secure home and went wandering.

After seventeen years of marriage I followed
a lovely gypsy girl deep into the forest
and before I knew it I was lost.[1]

Some wag has said, "The height of optimism in a man
is the hope that the next woman will be different." Middle-aged men may indulge in the fantasy that there is *a
woman somewhere who will give everything and ask nothing.*
In other words, he entertains the fiction that there is a
woman who will take care of his dependent needs the way
mothers take care of little boys when they are five or
six years old. On the other hand, middle-aged women carry
a sort of parallel fantasy that there may be *a man who
will take all she can dish out with tongue and tears and
come back lovingly.* This is what daddies do when little
girls kick and cry, but husbands almost never!

Another way that men at middle age act out is in denying
that they are limited financially. They might go on a
spending spree, buying things that mostly decorate the ego
such as clothing and automobiles. It could be a boat or
an airplane or some such "toy" that is out of reason. I
knew one fifty-year-old man who bought a whole new
wardrobe on credit and capped off the spree with a new
motorcycle.

What we are saying is that in both men and women
in middle age there is a tendency for a little extra "craziness" to come out. But just because the craziness boils
out, this doesn't have to be the end of the relationship
in marriage. Middle age finds a lot of unresolved feelings
from adolescence coming out for expression. "Middles-
cent" behavior is not unlike adolescent behavior. I'm not
trying to excuse such behavior that becomes so trouble-
some, but I'm trying to understand what is going on. When

mates can understand, they can cope with the crises a little better. They don't berate themselves for having failed. This self put-down tends to be more common in women than men. Maybe women are more introspective in these matters.

Significant Losses in Middle Age

Loss by Death

Not many of us reach middle age without losing someone close to us by death. There's one thing you can usually depend on, if death and loss in the past were not completed and resolved, we will deal with loss about the same way when it comes again. There is a way to break up the past patterns, and that is to decide you've suffered enough from old patterns, and that there is a better way . . . a way to properly grieve and finish the matter in our spirits. There are *stages* we go through in the loss of someone we love. These stages begin sometimes in prolonged illness of the person near us and may almost be all worked through by the time death comes. Let us get in touch with those stages.

Numbness is the first stage of grief. This is a kind of shock that is most natural. It serves a good purpose, because it keeps you from feeling the full impact of the truth while you go on doing what you have to do, such as making and carrying out plans for the funeral. There may be a feeling that you are not quite present to your body. There may be a loss of taste or even smell. On a sunny day, the sky might seem hazy, or you might feel slightly drugged or dazed. You can't quite clear your brain to think as you would like or remember something you struggle to bring to mind.

Shock is, in a psychological sense, a little parcel of death. Your body may feel half dead, and that is part of the process. You actually identify with the one who is dead, therefore, your living body is paying its sympathy to the one who died by this identification. The dead is with you at first, as it were, inside you, and it is most natural that you should lose your feeling since your love for the dead makes you take on their death. You may berate yourself for being the one who is alive and wish you could exchange places, giving your life to the one who is not so fortunate as you. So, your period of shock is often an attempt to take care of your own guilt at being the "chosen," that is, the one chosen to live. All the while you wish things were reversed between you and the dead, and this may be a final show of devotion and affection.

Shock is nature's anesthesia that shuts out other experiences and allows you to give attention to your grief. The practice of taking extra medication at this time makes one run the risk not only of shutting out experience, but it tends to shut out everything, including the grief; it tends to immobilize the entire mental process. The need at this point is one of putting aside everything except the grief.

Despair will easily follow shock, because in coming out of the numbness, there is the next stage of awareness: the one you loved is gone, you no longer have them as a part of your own life and existence. It is most natural that despair should awaken, because you realize the emptiness. At first, this is an emptiness you feel will never be filled, indeed, you would not allow it to be filled; not now at least. The person who died occupied a unique place and position in your life, and you will cling to that emptiness as an act of faithfulness to the dead. The despair puts you in touch with your own dependence, feelings of helplessness, and inability to change things as they are. You give yourself to a lot of pain; you might even make a vow never to give up the pain, yet that is a vow you will later need to resolve and rework, else the grief will be endless.

Nostalgia is a working of the human spirit to start a healing process. You know there is no more future, humanly speaking, with the dead. All that is left now is memories, so you take a journey into the past before the awful event brought its blow. You recall the good times together, the days when your lives were happily flowing in the same stream. The following will illustrate some of the process:

> A mother of forty-six lost her only son in an accident. She promised herself she would never give him up, and she tried to draw her husband into the same agreement. She railed out at her husband when he said how much he "loved" his son. She corrected him saying, "Don't ever say 'loved,' say you 'love' him!"
>
> Then she took out her favorite picture of the son in a football uniform. She went on to tell me how good he had been in sports. I gently reminded her that she said "had been." That was the breaking point, and she said acceptingly, "He doesn't play football anymore," and she wept.

We cling to the pictures of what was, and we begin to weep for what is no more. In nostalgia we can make too many promises to keep the past intact. This is where vows are taken to cling forever to the memories. We feel it would be a sacrilege to alter or forget. In the words of the psalmist grieving for his home: "If I forget you, O Jerusalem, let my right hand wither" (137:5, RSV). It is in that same spirit that parents often turn the room of a dead child into a life-chilling memorial.

The vow to hold to rituals of memory can bind a person in the stage of nostalgia so that no progress can be made toward resolving grief.

A woman of fifty came to talk to me about the grief over her husband who had died seven years before. I asked her after a session or two if Herbert had been the number one person in her life. She answered, "He not only was, but he still is number one." With this she told of how she not only tried to remember their life together, but she talked to him as she went about her housework.

Knowing she needed a shock in order to move ahead in her grief, I said, "I want you to be rewarded in your attempt to hold together your life with Herbert. I want you to go home now and have him greet you at the door with a kiss, then plan a party to have your friends in to celebrate the fact that you have him back." That was taking things too far for her! While she had remembered Herbert fondly, she couldn't cope with kissing him after seven years! She went away saying, "I really have to give him up." That was her beginning to move beyond the stage of nostalgia, some seven years late.

Anger or *resentment* tends to be the next step of grief. Most of us don't recall that as children we were resentful when we first learned the facts: "I knew not that they were born or that they should die," said Traherne. The shock about the limit of human life is a learned thing. It comes to the child with the force of an earthquake, and he resents such truth about others, because it is also truth about himself.

Say what we will, when a loved one dies, a part of our world collapses, and this produces frustration which is a forerunner of anger. Some people can't allow such pure expressions of anger as we sometimes hear. Yet they may get as far as a "Why?" or "Why did it happen to me?" or "Why now?" The feelings may come out in words like, "Why my father, when there are so many worthless people left alive?"

People who give answers to our anger do not help much—they are Job's counselors trying to defend God. These questions can no more be answered than you can tell a child why we are all mortals. Yet, if another human can hear our frustration, anger, and resentment and just allow us to be, with our mixture of feelings, we will be able to grow and move forward in our grief. If we are left having to hold these feelings inside, they tend to linger with us, only to crop out in ways that have no meaning even for us. We may get into a mad mood and stay there. But we don't solve grief by displacing feelings onto other situations. We need to let the pain be felt from the center of its cause in order to deal with it.

Acceptance is the stage where grief is finally reaching resolution. The failure to accept the death of a loved one, either in feelings or rituals, is to delay the final step. In feelings we might tell ourselves that our acceptance of death is a surrender, or an act that makes us responsible for the death. It is as if we did allow the event to be true, that we would be the cause of it all.

In yet another vein, our feelings might say that if we

don't hold on, nothing the person lived and died for will be kept alive. This can label us with the task of living out the life of the deceased in one fashion or another. It is an act of willing ourselves the place of justifying the life and death of the loved one.

Acceptance is really a surrender of sorts to the facts of existence and the limits of our own being human. The living cannot live for the dead without entering a dying process. If we cease to live out our lives in favor of living for the dead, we are no longer ourselves, but a replacement for someone else. Grief cannot then be resolved until we come back to the place where we left off.

We knew a lady of thirty-four who had vowed to take the place of her sister who died twenty-one years before. When she faced the psychological and spiritual demand that she accept her sister's death, she reached out and claimed the thirteen-year-old self, abandoned so long before. It was no easy thing for her to introduce her husband to a woman different from the one he married, nor was it easy for her to drop so far back that, in an emotional sense, she grew up with her children, being only slightly ahead of them when she abandoned her own self to become the self she imagined her sister would have been. This did not actually mean she became her sister, she only delayed being herself a long while.

When we consider the alternatives to acceptance of the death of a loved one, then acceptance seems right for the dead and the living.

In finally accepting the death of a person we loved, we are in position to take the positive step of investing the energies and emotions, once given to the one we lost, back into the community of the living.

The purpose of resolving grief is twofold, one is getting death out of our lives—the second is getting our lives out of death.[2]

We go ahead now to deal with various other losses. These stages or phases of grief may apply either in full or in part when other losses are concerned. I trust that no one will become so involved in defining the above stages that it will draw attention from your grief. It is much more important for you to allow yourself to be where you are than it is to push yourself along. A process of grief is like the digestive process—you give yourself to it rather than inspecting it.

Loss by Moving

Recently a friend asked me to see a middle-aged lady who was in very marked grief. The summary of the situation runs like this:

> This was a lady in the early fifties, her children were gone from home, and she had just moved to my city from the west; her husband worked for a national firm and had been transferred.
>
> Her grief took two expressions: one was over the loss or giving up of the dream home they had left (along with some dear friends); second, she resented deeply the house they now owned. In a very short time a wall crumbled, the chimney caved a bit, three different appliances broke, and the air conditioning went out. She said she felt the house had a curse upon it. Her grief was so heavy she almost talked her husband into taking early retirement so they could

move back where she felt at home.

In her grief she was in the stage of denial, so I not only permitted but encouraged her to go back through the process of returning to her former city. She had to face the fact that the home they had there had been sold. In addition, her husband would not have his "place" in the company with a comfortable income. Hence her friends would be on a different level. The more she pondered the different aspects of returning, the more she realized she had two options. She could accept where she was, or she could reject it. If she continued to reject it, she would continue to make everybody miserable. So she made a choice to move her spirit to the place where she had moved only her body a few months before.

Moving is a factor in modern life that has powerful overtones of grief and depression. If we suppress the feelings, we may stop our emotional growth. We may not move, but have grief over the neighbors who move away. We had the experience, a couple of years ago, of losing the very dearest neighbors after living side by side for twenty years. The grief didn't really hit me until they passed the act of sale on their house. It was that day that I knew we had lost them as neighbors for good, and there came a wave of grief and sorrow that it was so.

Loss by Divorce

It is not my aim here to make a judgment on divorce. Usually divorce has some markings of failure and self-examination. Any way you take it, divorce hurts children. They must go through the loss of a parent, usually the father.

Divorce spells the end of a relationship that began with hope, trust, love, and commitment. Now there is the awareness that it didn't work. Something is lost, or a hope never came into being. The grief at this point can be greater than loss by death. I have seen one person in such a situation cling to some hope of renewal of the relation, only to be hurt repeatedly. Where there is a funeral, there can be an easier finish to grief than where the judge of a court pronounces the end of a marriage.

Look at it another way: when two persons marry, they enter an understanding of making each other "number one." Divorce says that at least one of these persons wants his/her investment back; perhaps they want to invest it somewhere else, or have already done so. The grieving spouse tends to leave number one with the mate in some false hope that they will get the marriage back, while the truth may be to the contrary of their hopes and actions.

For the spouse in grief, I would urge a look at the facts. If the marriage is gone, then the business of the grief needs to be finished. That can only be done by choice and personal determination. Love cannot be kept alive on false promises or on imaginary dreams. If the mate has taken love and commitment away, this is not a time for trying to exist on memories of how it once was.

Love is a fire that burns in your fireplace to warm all who are in the house. Broken love can be a fire that burns down your house. It is not wrong to put out that kind of fire.

Loss of Employment

Middle age is a most critical time to lose your job. Have you ever been at a party when someone was asked what he did, and he replied that he was out of work? We hurry to fill the silence by telling what we did or what we hope to do. People are uncomfortable if you don't identify with a job of some sort. Ours is a culture that knows a man by the "hat" he wears . . . his employment.

In any case, the loss of a job is most disturbing, not only at the party, but most particularly inside the family, when that job spells food, rent, and transportation. There is grief over the loss, and there is discomfort throughout the family and community . . . grief over having lost your "place."

On the positive side, if you lose a job that is unpleasant, distasteful, dreary, or nonproductive, this may be the time and opportunity to do what you like. I knew a man who had held a good paying job for ten years but with the constant fear that he would be fired any month. He would have been better off losing that job or leaving much sooner.

Another area of great pain over the work situation comes when the middle-aged man goes without promotion for a long while. Things are further made painful if younger men climb past him, because they have some special education or skill. This accentuates that while you might have once been number one on the job, you are no longer in that position.

Other Losses

We cannot cover all of the examples of loss and grief. The important point is that you give yourself the right to feel the losses that you have—accept your feelings about them—claim them as your own—in your own time, at your own pace. Stay with them until you can finish your grief process.

It is all right to cry over the loss of your dog or cat, your canary or goldfish. I knew one man whose entire family went into grief because he lost an election. I knew another man who went into depression after he won an election—the new position called for more changes than he had anticipated. Some cry over the loss of a football game, others over the loss of a tennis match.

The loss of possessions can bring on grief, such as the loss of your house by fire, hurricane, or tornado. There are many such losses—an automobile in a wreck, an heirloom by breakage or theft, or maybe a special watch, vase, piece of furniture, silver, or jewelry.

I knew one lady who was in grief over being forty. Ten years later she was in grief over *not* being forty. So there is grief over lost time, places, things, persons, pets, or whatever. They all make marks in our spirits. We resist the changes they call for, but our hope is in the fact that we can lose and still invest again.

5. Claiming the Good Feelings

In order to have good feelings, you need to decide that you will not be controlled by bad ones. You need to give yourself permission to get with the good feelings that are a part of every human being who had a childhood. Dostoevski tells us of the importance of being in touch with our child of the past:

> Some good, sacred memory, preserved from childhood, is perhaps the best education. If a man carries many such memories with him into life, he is safe to the end of his days, and if one has only one good memory left in one's heart, even that may sometime be the means of saving him.[1]

This is no encouragement to be childish, but rather to allow that your feelings are very important, and it is important for you to let them have their rightful place in your life. This means that you use your intelligence to go with good feelings and take the lead to bring them forth in others. When you make somebody else happy, you will be happy for doing it. Again I'm not suggesting you give over to the control of feelings, good or bad; that would be irresponsible.

Mary Ben and I both grew up in the tradition that you

sat on feelings whenever there was any risk they would go out of control . . . either in joy or ecstasy or in sorrow and grief. So what I urge you to do, I tell myself. Mary Ben has made much more progress than I have toward breaking out into joy and celebration; she has much greater access to her feelings than I have toward mine. In fact, her freedom to feel her feelings makes me uneasy, and my uneasiness comes out as control of her, and control is what she doesn't want or need.

Where my generation went astray was in giving its chief reward to the one who was always responsible. This meant you were to stay on top of feelings, either positive or negative. Tears at a funeral were measured, a few were necessary to show your devotion; too many revealed a weak faith. On the positive side, we had our nearest thing to celebration at parties, usually on Saturday nights, with every reminder that God was looking through the windows of next day's sermon and Sunday School. To borrow a phrase from Karl Olsson, this will turn a "party" into a "social"!

The model person was the one who always remained in control, and the superior Christian was the one who policed the community to help others keep their emotions under control. He could help you with your grief by reminding you that neither God nor the dead would want you to cry. He could help with your unrestrained joy by reminding you that Christ was a man of sorrows. I must admit that this model was the one I affirmed in my youth and for several years after.

Now it is more important for me to be free than it is to be responsible . . . if I have to choose between them in my feelings. By that I mean the freedom to be a child, to laugh or cry without restraint, and the freedom to allow others to do the same.

It is not possible to be free with your sorrow while being restrained with your joy, nor can it be the other way around, full of joy but never in grief. There is a time to laugh and a time to mourn. Human emotions are like a piano: joy, peace, happiness, and celebration are the higher notes, while sorrow, depression, and grief will represent the lower range; but it takes them all to have an instrument that is right and beautiful.

Sometimes I am called on to help a person who cries all the time. I take this as a challenge to help them get the high notes unstuck, to help them discover that it is OK to laugh and express joy. Though I haven't tried the opposite for someone who laughs all the time, I wonder if the same principle applies.

At any rate, a lot of us find ourselves straying in the dark forest of human emotions at middle age; and we may need to allow the child in us to be reborn so that we can be in touch with all that we are. While this can be frightening, it also can be rewarding. Now we will deal with some positive feelings—joy, peace, and hope. There are others, yet these will constitute a start.

Joy

Joy is the child in the person; it is being in touch with the wonders of nature, the beginnings of life, the morning sun dancing through a misty spiderweb, or the cardinals chasing a grasshopper across the lawn. It is our response to the song and dance of creation, a rejoicing of the morning when nature stirs from the death of darkness to sing of regeneration. It is the timeless repeating of the seasons, of seedtime and harvest, of computerized bees buzzing the honeysuckle, or the unplanned and uncharted flutter of a butterfly.

The wonder of it brings a delight that I can feel the pulse of it all, be a part of the rhythm and cycle of nature, and still stand outside it enough to affirm that it is good, to reflect on its beauty, to paint it, or to sing about it.

The special joy of middle age is the joy of the afternoon, a joy I felt as a child in the fall of the year when we gathered the corn, cut the cane, and banked the potatoes against the coming winter. Our family, in response to what was ahead of us, molded into a single body to make our defense. Without the pressure and limit of time squeezing us, we would have missed many of the joys of togetherness.

Each passing day became a little shorter, telling us we must hasten our pace to get the wood cut, the kindling stored, the hogs killed, the syrup made, and the cotton picked. Old-man Winter would be along soon. That fact measured our steps and labors with a purpose and meaning that we wouldn't have known otherwise. The scene was enriched by the first bite of frost that colored the maples, sweetgum, and sumac, and put a sugary flavor in the persimmons. As I look back, it is also easy to get in touch with other feelings of celebration . . . the family table, our picnics, or the swimming hole.

Joy is not so much a thing that once was; it is a thing of the now, a feeling of celebration. Joy is my being revisited by my child of the past, or it is the awareness that all the children of the world have it now.

I repeat, joy is not a memory—it is a happening. You may recollect joyful experiences from the past, but joy escapes if you try to get back and recapture a past happiness. A joy is an individual, unique, different thing, different from every other joy and is not repeatable. Just as in nature where no two flowers are completely alike, so no two joys are ever the same.

A part of being a joyful person is the freedom to let a joy go in the trust that another will come when it will come. If you seek to control joy, it is like my experience of trapping a bluebird as a child. These birds were so much beauty and delight it seemed good to own one. But a bluebird in the hand, I learned, is not the joy of a bluebird in the bush. The bird needed to be in its element of freedom, not in the clutching captor's hand; and so it is with joy: to bind it is to lose it. Joy is more like the butterfly that flies an uncertain course but leaves a feeling of a floating bouquet whichever way it flits.

Yet joy does not come by pure accident; you have to look for it in order to find it, and you must have eyes to see it when it appears.

When the astronauts were first exploring the moon, those of us who followed them were aware of how dangers lurked at every turn, dangers of getting cut off from the precious oxygen, water, and food they took with them. Their hookup to the earth was so essential because all the elements around them seemed to press against them to suck up what they held to keep life going. I followed them about the surface of the moon with a kind of breathless fear—then I shared some of their joy as they trained their TV camera back on our blue-green ball in their sky, the earth. It was so small from out there, yet so beautiful. It made one feel it was itself a space capsule, and truly their mother ship, a ship that was spinning and flying in the ocean of the universe with many passengers, some of whom were learning for the first time that they clung to the only life-support system known to man.

Many of us got back from the moon adventure with a resolve to take care of this emerald, the earth, to love it, and delight in it. We took a vow not to forget how lifeless it is out there and how good it is to be here. I think a serious ecology was born in the 60s, because we fell in love again with "the good earth" as a result of getting outside and looking back.

Just as the ability to stand outside the earth may give us joy about the earth, so our ability to stand outside ourselves may give us the feeling of "ecstasy" which is derived from the Greek word for "stand outside." This is the symbol of *Jonathan Livingston Seagull,* getting above it all and getting the overview. We humans need to get out of our ruts of tradition, our slavery to habit and custom in order to find the ecstasy.

Raymond A. Moody, Jr., gives us the results of the ecstasy of people who experience clinical death.[2] Even in a crisis so great, we humans are not so bound to the body that we can't get outside enough to be ecstatic.

If we look for our joy at the end of the day, the end of the year, the sunset of life, or when the work is all done, the bills all paid, the grass all cut, the desk finished, the pain all healed . . . then we will let joy pass us by. We can stop where we are, call a halt to the process, and get above it or outside of it, and get with the good feelings of joy and celebration.

Perhaps you answer that there is too much sorrow in your life to be joyful, that joy would be out of place. My answer is that you can turn your sorrow into joy in the same way that nature can use dark clouds to beautify a sunrise or a sunset, but you have to be willing to back off from the clouds before their beauty appears.

Joy is what Karl Olsson calls "the party." He takes account of the miseries, the poverty, and the pain in the world but realizes that the first word of the good news is not a call to social work or some direct approach at reducing the misery, as important as this is. He says the invitation is not "to a freaked-out corner of the cosmos but to a new heaven and a new earth, which are really the old heaven and the old earth all dressed up for the party." [3] Hence the joy can't wait for all the problems to be solved.

We've taken much time to deal with joy in nature, but Karl Olsson touches the deeper truth that joy together with others, the "joy of relationship" is the sparkle. Our lives are bound up with others. The astronauts, homeward bound from the moon, were returning to a place of life, yet that life would be empty without belonging to wives, children, and friends. So they were coming back to the earth, but also to their places; their addresses in Clear Lake, Texas.

We, like the little child, do not long feel the joy until we want someone to see it with us. I suppose that is the contagion of joy: the more we share it, the more it increases! Joy says: "I called to see how you are feeling today." "Gee, that's a good piece of pie!" "Have a nice day," or "Thanks for the lift."

Joy is a breaking through, an interruption of our routine, a call to leave the business of the day to look at the business of the days.

A heavenly refrain, as it were, suddenly breaks off our other song; a joy which cools and refreshes us like a breath of wind, a wave of air from the trade wind which blows from the plains of Mamre to the everlasting habitations.[4]

Peace

Peace is another feeling we can have as a gift to our lives despite the troubled feelings around us. At middle age we become even more aware of the hazards of our journey, and if we choose, we can allow the turbulence to claim our power and rob us of peace.

Peace to the emotions is mirrored in the calm of nature before or after the storm. It is set in contrast to disturbance of wind or flood. Peace can be the inside of a snug cabin with the peals of thunder, the flashing of lightning, and the trembling of tall pines in the gale. We can even have a party on the block while we keep the hurricane watch; we huddle together against the enemy, and our huddling is warm and lively.

Peace is the assurance that what is, is all right, that what comes will be all right, too. This doesn't keep us from boarding up our windows, nailing down our shutters, and storing provisions against the storm. Yet, we know there are some storms that prevail against our best preparations, so there is a different order of preparation. We learn the meaning of peace in our assurance that no matter how many times we get engulfed, we will take the pieces left and build anew. We grow in the meaning of peace as we learn that we can get up from whatever crashes our ship, get our life jackets and swim out, each time learning something new and becoming better persons every time we start again.

Of course there are temptations to get away from the risk, to move to some area of calm and avoid encounter. This can be a kind of surrender to lack of growth and creativity. One man said, after the death of three persons he loved dearly, "I am afraid to get up and try again." He felt life was trying to break him rather than shape him, or he was afraid that further change might result in a break; it was his honest fear.

Peace is the knowledge and feeling that our earthly voyage is given to change. In the words of Sam Keen, "Our only security is our ability to change." [5] Yet, we might feel that change is too uncertain; we may be afraid of what change will do to us, we fear it will break us apart rather than reshape us.

We do not leave all the shaping to outside events; we take a hand in what comes out of each crisis, if we choose to do so.

Peace comes as the assurance that we grow and learn more from our mistakes than from our successes.

Peace is the assurance that failure is not so much our enemy as our teacher.

Peace is the awareness that pain is not so much our enemy as our opportunity to learn.

Peace is knowing that there are loving, helping hearts that can alert us and are willing to share our stress.

Even as we look back on our lives, we know that the places where we learned most were those where we got burned most (apologies to B. F. Skinner!). When we burn and don't learn, we have lost the gift of childhood, we may have lost our peace.

There are a lot of people out there who have no peace in that they feel or think they can't cope with life and its jolts. They are lost in the dark forest and can't again find the stars. But up there in the heavens is a pole star, something that is fixed, constant, and dependable for our emotional navigation. When we get lost and confused, I

think it is by our own choices, or by our refusal to wait
for the clouds to clear so we can see again. The will to
stay lost in the woods may be our way of getting rescued
because there are a lot of people whose lives are cast on
looking for lost ships or confused travelers. They get their
kicks out of being the ones who come to the rescue, but
they usually substitute a flashlight for the pole star. The
one being rescued is the victim or sufferer who gets his
kicks out of feeding the needs of the rescuer, or he gets
in trouble to accommodate the troubleshooter who thrives
on rescuing people.

Peace means you know the difference between being
a pilgrim and a wanderer (or a victim). One will travel
as far as the other, but the pilgrim takes charge of his
course, while the wanderer is at the mercy of uncertain
signposts or directions from villagers along the path who
have never themselves been out of the village. The wanderer becomes the victim of his own failure to ask the
question of what he is about or where he is going. The
pilgrim gets on with his journey because of his conviction
that he is on the way to joy and peace, hence he takes
every knockdown as a challenge to master obstacles on
his path while he keeps looking with the assurance that
the stars are there—somewhere!

Hope

If you lose your way in the "dark forest" of your journey,
you will come to the hope of finding a way out, or you
will come to despair. Despair is, in a real sense, the opposite
of hope. It literally means "to lose breath." On the other
hand, hope is a part of giving "inspiration" or new breath
to finding your way; it just might be the traveler's second
wind.

So there are two travelers in the forest, one who has despair of finding his way and the other who has hope. They are both at the same spot. Yet, they are in such different places. The despairer is getting near the end; the hopeful person is on the verge of a whole new experience. The despairer becomes the wanderer with life running out of its original zest. The person who has hope has his own renewal. In truth, if he never gets what he hopes for, he has already received that which hope gives . . . the good feelings of being OK while lost in the forest; this stands in sharp contrast to the hopelessness of despair.

Hope is the power of the future to shape the present. The simple hope for a scholarship or a medal will see an athlete undergoing all manner of rigors in training and diet in order to have a chance; what he hopes for makes him a different person now. A nation hoping for peace will shape its domestic and foreign policies to conform to the hope.

The despair of middle age is not uncommon because many of us set our hope only on getting to it, not through it. Perhaps we visit our relatives in the nursing home, and we shudder and tell our spirits we don't want to go down that path. We witness suffering, privation, or we panic over the thoughts of what inflation will do to our retirement dollars. In addition, there are prophets of doom over energy shortage, pollution, increased crime, racial violence, and drug addiction. While despair surrenders to these voices, hope does not change its course because hope believes in every manner of hidden possibility.

For hope "all things are possible." This means that a person of hope comes to expect surprise, or the unpredictable, even the unbelievable. The person of despair is in the rut of thinking the future has no openings, no options, no possibilities that he does not take into account from past experience. This is a neurotic position of only looking at one side of the picture. The possibility that anything can happen is the stuff that hope feeds on, a food that does not even exist for despair.

The very fact of unpredictable possibilities is what renders futurology a risky science. It must allow for unknown and unexpected turns in history and human behavior. Yet, by taking the growth rate of industry and population increase, the futurologist can make some needed projections for politicians and school boards.

The character of hope is not based on statistics, but on the goodness and rightness of what is coming; therefore the future shapes the now with meaning. In futurology things are reversed so that we take the now and extrapolate for one or two decades, hence shaping future actions on present trends. In hope we anticipate blessedness and goodness as our legacy, and we begin living off the interest in the now.

How can I suggest that you look for blessedness and goodness when you might have lived forty years with little of either? I suggest it because they are out there for eyes that can see and ears that can hear. If you decide that blessedness is a certain amount of income, you are not on the frequency to hear what your blessedness can be. It can come to you in any form or shape of pleasure or pain, but if it calls on you to grow, share, communicate, and relate, then perhaps you can hear.

In conclusion: It seems that these three emotions, while being in the present, have a relation to time. Joy is fed partly from the springs of childhood. Hope is fed partly from a persuasion that the future is both powerful and friendly. Peace is the assurance that the waves of the storm behind us or before us will not destroy us.

The good feelings may be our richest heritage. A lot of our resources are spent on drugs, alcohol, and medication in order to help us stop feeling what we feel in order that we might tell ourselves a lie about ourselves or our situation. These pills and props help us get outside that we may have a false ecstasy, but "coming back home" is the hangover.

There are better ways to get outside than getting "high," and the spaceship for the trip is the Truth. When we commit to Truth, it usually cuts us loose from much of the baggage and garbage that would keep us earthbound all of our days.

6. Dealing with Feeling

The way we feel is as unique as each of us is different. The set of feelings that we bring to middle age has been building through all of our lives. With the change of lifestyle, children growing up, loss of parents, we have opportunity to think about ourselves for a change. Women may feel a need to break the mold of reacting to situations that they learned in earlier years. They make a claim for feelings of self-worth in many ways. Some get into the job market because that paycheck feels like affirmation, approval. The ability to help bear the expenses of a large family helped me feel like I was contributing in a worthwhile way.

Carl Jung describes some middle-age behavior in which women have fantasies much as they did in adolescence. They daydream of magic men who can meet their need for romance and approval. Sometimes that Prince Charming will match up with the dream by materializing . . . in the form of a co-worker, therapist, or doctor. A whole set of fantasies is laid on him and turns him into the answer to her daydream.

There is time in middle age to develop talents that have been neglected because of first choice careers of homemaking, mothering.

My sister, in middle age, went back to college to pursue

her education; a cousin got her degree in nursing education. One of my friends is enjoying a successful second
career in the real estate market; another is a banker. Still
another friend who enjoyed going to camp in her youth
has fun helping direct summer camp for children. Still
another friend has bought a summer home in Maine and
has become an expert on the flora and fauna of that area.
During the teacher shortage of the turbulent sixties, after
our youngest child enrolled in school, I went back to school
as a public schoolteacher. I will limit my comment. We
did put the earnings from those years to very good use
because our children were in college. I did have isolated
experiences with promising students that enrich my feelings
of that involvement. But: being in the revolution in the
schools during the sixties and early seventies would make
a story for another book.

I've referred primarily to positive feelings that come in
middle age as I've spoken of my friends. Sometimes negative, frustrating feelings must be dealt with. In *Grief Observed*, C. S. Lewis says, "No one ever told me that grief
felt so much like fear. I am not afraid but the sensation
is like being afraid." [1] He was referring to his reaction
to the death of his wife. This gave me the realization that
deep negative feelings are hard to classify. Hurt, grief, loss,
rejection, guilt, misunderstanding result in a feeling of low
esteem. They whittle away at your self-confidence and feel
like a putdown. My experience seems to be that unresolved
bad feelings are a source of depression that cries out for
understanding. In working for insight into my own feelings
I will tell of an experience of grief of death as a four-year-
old. This year I awakened from sleep and wrote of it in
a journal and felt it as a recent event. I share:

I'm dealing with my feelings about losing my little three-year-old brother. My parents were living with my grandparents. Johnny Boy was spending a few days with our aunt. I was shocked awake in the night with outcries of grief. My little brother, my aunt, uncle, and two cousins had been burned to death in their home. I remember going out onto the porch of Granddaddy's country home. The moon was shining very brightly. A stranger had come in his car from out of the night to bring the death news. I remember my impression of the beauty of the earth, as contrasted to the storm of weeping, wailing, groaning that I was seeing and hearing.

From that point I have no recollection of the event. After I became an adult, I mentioned to an aunt that I have no recollection of the mass funeral that followed. She answered, "You did not go to the funeral. You had a boil on your leg and someone kept you at home."

Thinking of what I feel is a concept that I'm working on in middle age. The pain and fear from that early experience seemed to have given me the resolve to make up the loss of my brother to my parents by being a good girl, a model child. My model of "trying to be good" carried through to wifehood and motherhood.

I have seriously considered going to a professional counselor to talk. That would have been helpful years ago. For now, I am satisfied that I have recalled my grief and broken a pattern of suppression. Growth experiences such as I've experienced at Laity Lodge, involvement in group personal growth experience here in the counseling center at Southern Baptist Hospital, lectures, and books have helped me interpret what is going on in my life. My theological concepts that began in my parents' home and have been a part of the dialogue of our own home have made me feel happy in the present and secure in my faith for the future.

In our family we have worked on cultivating a sense of humor. From Myron's mother he received the gift of looking for comedy in life's dourest moments. We have tried to get outside our bad moments and look for the dialectical "on the other hand." As a result, our children have a lively sense of humor and gift of wit. I mention this to say that having fun has claimed a healthy part of our attention.

Feeling like a peer has been a challenge in relation to authority figures. A few days ago a police car followed me down the street with lights whirling. A stern young officer left his vehicle, approached my car. Looking down through the window, he addressed me, "Your driver's license, please."

I handed it over.

"Mrs. Madden, didn't you know you were going the wrong way on a one-way street?"

"Well, no, I didn't. I didn't see a sign. It must be a new sign. Anyway I don't live in this part of town. I just drove in from the country to pick up my husband's mail."

I hoped he'd realize that it was a simple mistake. His buddy waiting in the car joined him.

I signed the ticket.

He kept my driver's license.

I felt putdown.

Then I checked the street again for a sign. Sure enough I had driven two blocks as it stated on my ticket "against a one-way street." That would cost me ten dollars a block for that infraction. It comforted me to remember Myron's logic that went:

"If you spread the price of a traffic ticket over a whole year, it's only a few cents a day. You can afford it!"

Since I had tried to learn how to feel in my formative years from authority persons and had patterned my responses on what I saw, I repressed negative feelings. Realizing that, they are a part and parcel of total involvement with living. I'm trying to claim and learn what negative as well as positive feelings are saying to me.

SECTION III
GETTING SOME ESSENTIALS TOGETHER

7. Getting Your Numbers Together

Many people lost in the woods at middle age are advised that the way out is to decide *what* is most important.

Let's not deal with *what*.

Let's start with *who*.

The chief meaning of life centers in who, not what.

The "whats" are easier to grade when the "whos" are settled.

Your Number-One Person

If someone asks you who the most important person is in your life, how would you answer?

Perhaps it is better to begin with a case history in personal counseling. We will call the man and woman Ralph and Jane; I saw only Ralph.

Ralph is a fifty-two-year-old man who wanted to talk things over; his wife had asked him to leave since she planned to divorce him. He hoped that in counseling he would find some magical formula for getting a second chance in his marriage, because he loved his wife dearly. They had been married thirty-one years and had six children. Ralph was an engineer by profession, he had not before sought help. Jane, in the meantime, was seeing a psychiatrist three times weekly on income from her father's estate. Psychiatric counseling had been in progress, off and on, for some six years.

After we got acquainted, I asked Ralph if Jane was his number one person; that is, was she the most important person in existence, the one he would take the bullet for. He said without a shadow of a doubt she was number one.

I then asked him to tell me if he was or had been number one to Jane. He didn't answer quickly, but thought a while. Finally he said, "I haven't been number one to my wife since my first child was born" (twenty-nine years before).

After he said that, he wondered if he had ever been number one to her. He pondered and speculated that her father was number one when they married. Maybe for a year she was able to give Ralph some real affection, but number one? It was doubtful.

When Ralph came for his second session, I wondered what he had decided. He had worked hard with the idea of giving and exchanging number one, and he realized he could work all his days trying, but Jane just didn't or couldn't give him first place. With that awareness, and the sure knowledge of how much pain there would be for him and also how little reward, he declared himself free.

He was determined to take back his investment of affection in Jane and put it with someone who would also make him their most important person. He knew this would not be easy; I reminded him he would likely have to go through the greatest grief of his life.

The last thing Jane expected was for Ralph to give her up. For a time she almost made him think he could have her affection, yet he thought this would be her reaction; he was persuaded that she was not really sincere.

I don't know where Ralph will go with his life, I just know that at present he is in intense pain and grief. Part of that pain is over the fact that he didn't begin his marriage on the full assurance that wife had truly left father and mother that they might be "one flesh." He is wandering in his own wilderness, and that has to be, in order that he can fully grasp the fact that, Jane, his one-time hope for a lifetime, is out of reach. She can't be the one for whom he lives, no matter how he tries. He must reconcile his hopes for the future with his grief of the past.

Before Ralph can go on to decide "who," he has the problem of "not-who" . . . and that fills him with frustration and much pain. He knows he has to complete his wilderness wandering until he finishes his grief. Otherwise he might, in his loneliness, rush to fill his pain. He might repeat the familiar pattern of giving the number one position to someone who does not give him the same position.

He came to realize also that the effective handling of number one place comes in an exchange. If you give it in order to get, you will not likely get it.

Ralph speculated that the exchange of number one likely takes place as a great risk. You ask someone with the knowledge that if you are refused, you will be, for a time, wiped out. He spoke of it as "gift" or it is "nothing." Literally, it is a promise of one's self to another self. That other self always has an option to accept or reject.

The Numbers Game

Ralph is an example of one who gave number one

without getting it but, at least he assumed he got it. This is the situation with a lot of persons, men or women. More often the problem centers around a son who can't turn mother or sister loose in the deeper feelings when he comes to the altar. The reverse is true of the bride who is given away by a father who keeps his fingers crossed.

There are many persons who give their number one to another person without being made number one by that person. I feel that most do it unknowingly or at least without taking the honest look. They might just assume too much. For example, a certain young woman fell in love with a professional man knowing he put his profession ahead of everything else in life. (A "what" ahead of any "who" . . . the curse of the professional marriage!) At any rate she just knew she could earn first place with him by loving him and furnishing what it would take to get him through school. She would work night and day (and did) taking a job, and doing all the housekeeping to give him every assurance she was there to love him. How could a man refuse to give such a woman first place? You've already got the answer . . . you can't earn it, no matter what you are prepared to pay. It is gift or it is nothing.

You also know the rest of the story. As soon as the man got his education and was ready to move up in professional (and financial) circles, he dropped his wife like the first stage of a rocket. She succeeded in getting him launched and was no longer useful. His profession remained more important to him than persons, though he is supposed to be in a profession that helps persons!

The other side of the numbers game is that of *getting number one without giving it.*

This may mean you play a desperate game if you make someone believe you are going to give them the number one place but only after they have come through first.

Another game is that of acting "as if" you will give it away to someone when you are unable to release such a position to another. It frightens you to think of making someone more important to you than you are to yourself. What if they prove unworthy, unstable, or unfaithful?

Someone argued that you are not even called on to love anyone more than you love yourself, quoting the Bible, "Love your neighbor as yourself." My answer is that I feel you will love your mate, or whoever your number one person is, more than your neighbor.

It is not our purpose here to establish whether we are talking about another person (number one) as the most important person besides yourself or including yourself. That would be a book in itself. Only you can answer it anyway.

It seems easier for the prince, the professional sportsman, the rich, the powerful, or the distinguished person to get to be number one without giving it. Perhaps most Cinderellas will be contented to be number ten while giving number one position to Prince Charming. So, instead of being his number one, their song is that they "want to be in that number." The Prince Charmings are in the game of collecting number ones.

Change the scenery a bit. You are on stage for a season, you are popular and in great demand by your public. You haven't decided who your lover will be, but there are dozens of hopefuls out there. In this way you can easily get into the numbers game of getting full commitment from someone only by indicating your interest in one of the many hopefuls. If you are clever, you might get a dozen or so number one commitments without giving yours away at all. I have only one real question: What will it finally cost you?

What does it cost you to be number one to more than one?

Hard Decisions on Number One

I asked a man of forty-four what it was going to cost him to be number one to two women: his wife and a woman in his business. He came all the way back from England to work on the question, though actually he hoped to remain astride the fence; throwing his number one feelings now to this side, now to that, depending on which woman was withdrawing at the time. He gave it to the one who was angry with him, hence he was always in a state of anxiety and misery.

I told him he reminded me of a little magnolia tree that Mary Ben planted. It has developed a fork from the ground, so I told him that in the fall, I was going to make a decision about which side was larger and straighter, and in order to have a tree later, one side would have to go. I told him the "axe was laid at the root of the tree" and if he couldn't use it, he couldn't get out of the woods. He couldn't do so at the time; he will have to wander some more and hurt some more. He will have just so much time before one or both of the women decide that they will settle the matter.

A Closer Look at Number One

There are all kinds of problems and questions raised by this concept. The following are some general assumptions that we can make.

We can allow ourselves to be made number one by more than one person at a time.

We cannot give number one position to more than one person at one time.

If a person is your number one love, they are the most important person in your life.

You can make someone your number one person and still not be number one to them.

You can allow someone to make you number one person and remain free from giving them first place in your affection.

We can make a task, an honor, or a profession more important than a person.

We can remain number one in devotion to ourselves without giving it to anyone else.

We can spend a lifetime trying to get someone to make us number one without success.

We can give number one place to someone, hoping in the meantime to earn the reciprocating favor of their number one.

Number one place cannot be earned!

Some of us have difficulty giving number one importance to the person who gives us number one importance (a case or two later).

The happy mature position: giving number one place and getting in return number one place from the same person.

The game of politics: getting number one promises from as many as possible, while giving up as little in return as is necessary, to keep the game going.

Following this reasoning, just as you could not have two number ones, so it is with all other numbers. Properly understood, if you are related to a thousand people altogether in some way or other, and all the data is fed to a computer for evaluation, they would come out from one to a thousand, no two having the same number.

Everyone Wants Somewhere, in Some Way, to Be Number One Person

One of the most painful utterings I ever heard was from a man who said, "I've never been number one to anyone in my life." In addition, he despaired that he could ever be. All that was left for him was to remain number one with himself, and that was not a happy prospect for his future.

We operate from a rather natural need to be number one. How many fans claim it every year for their football teams! If not in sports then we claim it in what we sell or buy; in our candidate for office; or we bestow it on the doctor or lawyer we patronize; we want to be and to possess number one.

In my observation, the gambler tends to be the person who didn't get to be number one where he wanted it most, so he feels fate owes a special place to him. He refuses to learn that it is not "in the numbers" of fate to give it to him. So he keeps throwing the dice or spinning the roulette wheel. He is determined to wrest his reward from the hand of fate. What didn't come early from mother must surely be concealed in the skirts of chance.

It seems to be a human trait that we are always and in every place on the alert for how we might get some position of preference. Our little three-year-old granddaughter Sara cornered Mary Ben and asked, "Mona, do you love me best?" I might have to keep an eye on that situation! A question like that could start a conspiracy in the family! But that illustrates how early in life it gets important to be number one.

An Honest Struggle with the Issue

I have friends that went through this struggle at middle age and found their way. It went something like this.

The couple, Jim and Sue, were in their early forties. Their oldest son had just gotten married. Sue wanted to discuss it. We had coffee together where she worked. I led off with a question, "Now that number one son has married, are you going to let him remain number one person?" I asked because I knew she held that son most dear of all people. She replied, "No, he took his back, so I'm going to take mine back." I asked if she would give it back to her husband Jim. She wasn't sure, she said Jim never knew he had lost it. (Which I doubted!)

Three weeks later I saw Sue and she flashed a button she had found at a dime store with the words "You are number one." I asked her what she planned to do with the button. She planned to give it to Jim. But the transaction was a heavy one, because when she gave it, she was sick for three days.

Middle age is a time to make this kind of decision. Jim and Sue had married in their late teens; they had to regroup to make sure they had the will and strength as well as the commitment to continue the journey together.

Various Levels of Number One

The situation of Jim and Sue brings up another consideration: that of the different levels of number one place.

In Sue's devotion to her first son she had gone beyond the usual limits of parental devotion, making number one child her number one person. The son was fortunate that he could break through and take what he had given to his mother and transfer it to his bride.

A parent can make a child number one child without making him number one person.

A child usually makes a parent number one person somewhere along the way. If the parent does not reciprocate, the child is in an easier position to fall in love and get married. If parent and child become the most important to each other, there is more strain and a sense of rupture or unfaithfulness when number one is taken back and given to a lover. This is the background problem where a parent shows his or her disapproval in regard to the child's selection of a mate. This is where a parent often refuses to "bless" the marriage of a son or daughter.

There are other levels. You may have a number one in many different areas without making that one the most important to you. For example there may be a number one hairdresser, a number one dentist, a number one doctor, a number one minister, decorator, or mechanic. This list can be almost endless, but the people in these roles usually are number one to you in their function, not in their person.

Number One in Suspension

Earlier we referred to the young woman who lost her husband, the professional man. She finally managed to take back her number one place and made herself most important. She remarked that this was a most uncomfortable position. Another woman lost her husband by death. In taking back her investment in him, there were four persons bidding for her primary affection. Her two parents; her grandmother, and her son. All made her the focus of their lives and interest and poured out their devotion in expectation of becoming most important to her.

The situation of death and divorce may find a person holding the feelings for the one lost in a most guarded way. Some say "I will never love again," yet they have to decide if they are going to invest it again or run the risk of becoming bound up within themselves.

If someone has lost his number one person, it is the usual thing to take that investment of feeling back. Where does it go, then? It can go to a child, a parent, or it can remain with the self. If it goes to a child, there is the risk that the child will be overloaded with expectation. If it goes to a parent, the parent will not be able to carry it as long as we would hope. If we keep it ourselves, we are heavy on our own hands. It wants to go to someone who is free to give us love in exchange.

The Payoff Number

One man loved a woman very much but she didn't return the love, but gave it to someone else. In like manner the woman did not get first place with the man she made first, but held a lesser place with him. Most of us know many stories like that where there is a kind of chain: love being given but not received from the one who got it.

A couple in their late thirties wanted to try to save their marriage. Very simply the husband had another woman. His wife finally decided to call it quits. The husband promptly left the affair and came home. The wife took him back. They settled in for a time, but he got into another affair. She repeated the past cycle.

She finally sued for divorce saying that as long as she made her husband number two, he could make her number one, but when she made him number one, this left him free to gamble with his position.

She taught me a truth about her husband which is sometimes true about many relationships: some seem to be unable to give and receive firstness with each other; or at least one of the couple has the problem. We have already commented that maturity is the condition where two persons can give and receive first place with each other and are able to stabilize their relationship.

At middle age the boat has already sailed through some troubled waters. We are not adolescents anymore, our decisions can be based more on our persons than our passions. Commitment and decision can be the ground of the relationship. Now we may be mature enough to accept that we didn't marry a star or some person of fame, power, or glory in our twenties. That is now all right, where we are is all right, there are other considerations.

Mary Ben has referred to a speech in which I teasingly said that I could accept everybody as they were, but held out for her to change. She took it as a putdown. I suppose that was my attitude for years. God only knows how I tried to change her. Now I happily see her claiming her right to be herself no matter what, and that is beautiful.

Change for Mary Ben or change for myself is not the first article in our agreement to live together, but rather commitment. That commitment comes on the heels of a lot of hurt, and we know there will be more. There is a commitment to be straight about bad feelings, putdowns, frustrations, and doubts. We try to take seriously what we have said here about the fact that getting through a crisis makes you stronger. We feel it makes a marriage stronger and more likely to endure.

I am not trying to lay a heavy weight on anyone by dealing with this examination of number one. Yet, I do feel that it is a useful method of examining where you are. It is a tool to ask yourself if that's where you want to be.

I go back to the first case in this chapter reminding you of the beautiful guy, Ralph, who wanted to save his marriage. Yet, he couldn't do it with integrity. Too much water had gone under the bridge. I am not citing him to bring judgment on anyone. If his wife had had this concept, she might realize that there are no more number ones out there for her. Then she might take Ralph for the same reason that Eve took Adam . . . there were no other choices! She might even come to reward him for all those years she put her main emotions in other people or places. She has struggled in a thousand ways to change her husband; she might now let herself wake up to the fact that neither husbands or wives can mold the other into perfection.

In the *Birthmark*, Nathaniel Hawthorne has a chemist husband set about to make just the right potion to remove the birthmark on his wife's face, a birthmark that really enhanced her beauty. He finally got the right mixture; the birthmark disappeared just as she expired! That story is a commentary on me. It is a comment on the lot of humans who in our unblessedness, go about to change the wonderful world of people around us. We try to bring about change in them, rather than change in ourselves . . . and to love as is!

8. Getting Mind and Body Together

We use the terms *emotional health* and *mental health* as if they are about the same. They are no more the same than the concepts of *body* and *mind.* One is where we feel, the other is where we think. One of these spheres can't be sick without making the other sick. They are both positive or neither is positive.

Mind and Body in Contrast

We begin by affirming that mind and body are concepts; they are not divided, but they are interrelated. The mind is not superior to the body. We have for many generations referred to the emotions as the area of the "lower" nature in man while we have thought of reason as that part of man approaching the Divine. This kind of thinking leads to poor mental health because in doing it we are feeding the mind on untruth. It leads to poor emotional health also because in making the mind a tyrant over the body, we tend to get rebellion in the feelings against this abuse.

At middle age we deal a bit more with the importance of emotional health simply because feelings tend to come to the surface more at this time. There may be a catching up now on hurts that have been driven underground for a decade or two.

In order to have mental health, we need to understand

a thing, a feeling, or a process.

— — —

In order to have emotional health, we need to *claim* a feeling or a pain and make room for it in the place where it belongs.

— — —

The body, through the emotions, is our contact with nature and all the physical world.

The mind is our contact with the man-made world, that nonphysical world of thinking, explaining, interpreting, and understanding.

— — —

The mind is set on classifying or explaining.

The body and the emotions are in need of being owned.

— — —

The mental process is one of sorting out, separating, dividing, and untangling.

The emotional process is one of letting the "lion and the lamb lie down together," of leaving the "wheat and the tares" to grow alongside each other.

— — —

The mind must give a thing a name and thus make it different from all other things.

The emotions are blind to many differences.

— — —

The mind says, "I can only love this particular man."

The emotions say, "All men are alike"; they have no great differences.

— — —

The mind says this thing is more important than that.

The emotions say any one thing is as important as any other thing, or whatever is on top of the need list is most important.

– – –

The mind says the future is important.
The body says there is nothing but now.

– – –

The mind says of the feelings, "Some of you are unwelcome in my house."
The emotions say, "We do not know good and bad, we all belong here."

– – –

The mind says, "I want the *light.*"
The body says, "I prefer the *warmth.*"

– – –

The mind wants to take everything apart.
The body wants to lump it all together.

– – –

The mind is the daylight where the trees, flowers, shrubs, weeds, and posts stand out as separate things.
The emotions are the night where everything is merged.

– – –

To the mind, *cold* is measured on the thermometer, or it comes as a snowstorm.
To the emotions, *cold* is a friend turned away.

– – –

To the mind, *warm* is a sunny day.
To the emotions, *warm* is an open smile.

– – –

The emotions feel a feeling.

The mind explains a feeling: a feeling is pleasant or unpleasant; it is common or unique; it is acceptable or unacceptable; it is caused by this or that; it lasts for such and such a time.

— — —

The emotions come first, the child feels things for three to four years before the questions of what or why.

The mind develops as a light to shine in the emotional darkness . . . and to look for snakes!

— — —

The emotions of the child are when "the earth was without form and darkness was on the face of the deep."

The mind is the command to let the light shine upon the darkness and bring words to the mass and tangle of unworded experience.

— — —

The emotions are bound to the mother . . . earth, who says, "All things are yours."

The mind is the father who separates and singles out and classifies and cautions . . . "If you eat this one you will die."

These polarities between mind and body have been there from the beginning; they are a part of what it means to be human.

When the emotions can't finish a process, some things will be forced down as "lumps" for later digestion.

The same is true of the mental process; what we can't understand is pushed down with a promise to think about it tomorrow.

Friedrich Nietzsche once said that a man must digest his experiences just as he digests his meats, even though he has some tough morsels to swallow. Middle age can be a time to digest the lumps we have forced down in both the emotional area as well as the mental. It can be a time for claiming the emotions that are snarled, as well as a time for seeking honest answers to the questions that remain unsatisfied because of half-truths we give ourselves. Let us look at the lumps in both body and mind.

The Lumps of the Emotions

The greatest discovery of Sigmund Freud about us humans is that in the early years the child gets the notion that some of his wishes and feelings are so terrible that if they became known it would lead to his murder or mutilation. He gets the idea that something of what he feels is totally unacceptable to parents, therefore, this material must be put out of his mind and thoughts forever. Hence the term *repression.* Repression is the act of banishing these feelings for all time. I am quite doubtful if Freud was right that all feelings have to do with sex, but I think the general principle of repression holds true. When we bury unacceptable feelings inside ourselves, we go through life with some unfinished business.

After we learn to repress, we later need to learn to unrepress. It is a common need of adults, any age, to allow life to soften and mellow relationships, and this nudges the repressed fears of childhood out of the closets of the past. These "ghosts" from the past frighten us into thinking we can't be accepted; then some loving, caring person breaks the spell of fear with their love. This in turn makes it easier for us to love ourselves when we realize our ghosts do not frighten others.

While we may not be able to fully accept ourselves, relationships help us to view ourselves as not singular in having problems. We become aware of the humanity of mankind. All persons have hurt, no one comes from a perfect background; there is conflict with children; disappointments are the common lot of everyone. Relationship to another, comradeship gives courage to accept unresolved feelings. A friend, counselor, or minister can be a guide to help us explore our personal pain.

A surprising truth is that weakness in one person can be the very point at which another can give affirmation. Identification can be a common bond. Sympathy with pain is as strong a tie as affirmation for strength. Our perfections threaten, our weaknesses unite us with our brothers. I am commenting on the nature of personal relationship. I am not dealing with "ought" or "should" and saying we ought to sin that our friends may be comforted. Repressed material in the form of a lump—dark repressed material is a part of all of us. We carry it around with us—keep it secreted—keep it hidden as though the world will explode in wrath if it is released. "Should" and "ought" control our reaction in that area. We allocate energy to hold it down. As mature adults, we deliberately release this energy in another direction by dealing with our own wounds in a way that allows them to heal. Unless we do this we have unfinished business in our spirit.

At any rate, we all carry around feelings that hold themselves in a kind of inner dungeon or prison. This was originally brought about by the fact that as children we really misunderstood our first brush with "thou shalt not." We imposed the death sentence upon ourselves saying, "If he or she learns my thoughts (or feelings) they will surely bring my life to an end."

It is pretty natural to take a "lump" of dark, forgotten material and lug it round with us as the thing that must be kept hidden lest all the important people reject us. This is a lie we tell ourselves long after we know better.

Now feelings don't like to be told to sit down anymore than a child likes such a word from the teacher in a classroom. Yet, they get orders like that every day and sometimes all day along. Here is an example. A superior officer in the Army told me to stop what I was doing. He didn't ask me for the good reasons why I was doing it, nor did he give me the Army's reasons why I should stop. He just said, "Stop!" My feelings were greatly wounded, especially because I felt I was doing good for a lot of people. But the United States Army in toto was represented by one colonel and the word was *stop*. There was absolutely no choice but to accede and say, "Yes, sir."

But that was not the end of the story. That was the end of the happening. But night came on, and there was time for sleep. I went to bed with all that frustration, humiliation (the order had been given in the presence of two or three other people), and if I could have admitted it to myself, just pure rage. All those feelings were there, but they couldn't speak. In the middle of my sleep a quarrel was provoked between the Colonel and me, only he was not a colonel, just a private civilian. You wouldn't believe how unmerciful I was in pounding him to a pulp with my fists. Even though that dream was some thirty years ago, I still recall the good feelings of relief it brought.

The body and feelings seemed to say: "You are in the Army, the word of a superior officer is law. You don't talk back, give excuses or answers, you just obey and be quiet." This is the picture of the power of society and reason to put the feelings under wraps (and this is not all bad). I made a choice and put the feelings down. When I went to sleep, the feelings sort of went at it this way:

"Now Mr. Mind, you've had your way, you made me take all this stuff and choke it down. I want you to take it back now because I'm dumping all that garbage back on your side of the street." The body used the mind to get a make-believe fight started so at least some of the unspent emotions could be discharged.

Mind and body go to war when the issues are as bold as we have just described. But this is not such an extraordinary case. This sort of process goes on all the time. What the body wants most is to sleep. It can't sleep, because it keeps getting disturbed by the garbage that was thrust in during the day before. The body dispatches the mind to the task of cleaning up the mess it made. For example, the body may have the mind tell it all kinds of falsehoods because the body wants to get its rest but keeps on being interrupted by the anxieties the mind forced upon the feelings in the waking hours. For example you did a foolish thing and spent more money than you could afford on a big dinner. In your sleep the anxiety might be solved by your dream helping you dig in the earth, and find coins in the ground like gravel. The end result says: "Stay asleep, you weren't so foolish, there's plenty of money."

The lumps in the emotions that give most trouble are the ones that leave us with every manner of bad feelings, especially those of guilt, anxiety, shame, and worthlessness. These are the "child" within us speaking loudly. If we listen and believe these inner voices, they take away our power as adults.

If we did not have some of these voices inside, we could not relate to other adults, because everyone has some of them. These inner voices make us all afraid to risk relationship: each of us is afraid the other will reject us. We feel this because we begin with the assumption that we

have most of the bad feelings . . . and that others wouldn't
know about such feelings. It is time we made a turnabout
and claimed all these feelings in the way a father or mother
assumes responsibility for their children. If we wait for
the "children" to set the mood, there will be little happiness
in our houses or in our bodies. We can declare our place,
our strength, our rights as adults, and be done with these
"childish hobgoblins" as Socrates once told us.

Lumps in the Mental Life

Charles Kettering once said, after many years of research, that if he knew why grass was green, he would
likely be the smartest man alive. We don't know much!
We are told that the atoms in a piece of paper are as
far apart relatively as the planets in the solar system, and
that the atom is further divided into electrons and protons
that are thousands of times smaller than the atoms as a
whole. I simply don't understand enough to make sense
out of it.

I can understand that the earth rotates around the sun,
that my food digests most times when I eat it, that my
car runs when I press on the accelerator. I do not know
why.

The mind is such that it gives itself some kind of answer
to the many whys, yet those answers are temporary. They
are guesses based on what little we know, and they serve
us until we get a better answer. Answers ought to keep
on getting closer to truth, yet they may never be perfected
so we can close the book and walk away.

We adults tend to lead children to think that the answers
all come when you grow up. That is often our dodge to
keep our clay feet covered. For example, a lady called
me about her four-year-old granddaughter wanting to

know all about what happened to her grandfather at the funeral. She said, "Should I tell her all about what happens to you when you die, about heaven and what it is like?" My reply was, "If you know, go ahead and tell her!" And I added that I would like to be the next one to hear it.

We get lumps in our mental life when we tell ourselves falsehoods, things that are untrue and unreal, or when we build our lives on prejudice, falsehood, or untested assumptions. Yet, even those things will support our early growth provided our first loyalty is to the truth. In that way we can later tear out the old forms like the contractor who tears away lumber after the concrete has been poured.

There were so many things I swallowed on authority from my culture, answers that will not support my growth as an adult. That is a common experience, I suppose, of us all, to take in beliefs and assumptions about Jews, blacks, and Roman Catholics that keep us from being open to them as human beings. The truth haunts us if we try to deal with any other human as less than human; we end up with lumps that block our growth toward fuller humanity.

Truth is for those who can hear it; it is not exclusive, racial, biased, or limited. It is open, questing, searching, sharing, and relating. To be sure there are many truths, but they all flow toward the big stream of truth that becomes what the apostle John called the "river of the water of life."

The mental lumps are those false assumptions that we made about the reality of life. The task of updating and correcting is an ongoing process as we acquire knowledge.

An example of this: one of our children heard a loud blast from an explosion a mile or so from our home. This came at a time when TV was feeding him the tension between the United States and Cuba. His immediate question, quick as a flash, "Is that the bomb?" He was interpreting what he was hearing on the local scene by what he was hearing on the national scene. For him, in that moment, the whole world might be engulfed in war, all coming from a noise down the street.

The story of Henny-Penny is one that illustrates what we are saying. She sent about shouting that the sky was falling, only to learn later that the matter was as local as acorns that fell on her head. But Henny-Penny acted on what she believed to be the truth and sounded the general alarm that the universe could no longer be trusted.

Let's illustrate this problem another way. The people of the earth believed for centuries that the earth was flat, not round. Earlier they believed the earth was the center of the universe with sun and moon alike rotating around the earth. They believed those things, and they acted on them even though they were not true. They built their actions around false assumptions, and they were afraid to sail the open seas lest they fall off the end of the earth. They took what seemed to be true and defended it as the truth.

Men everywhere greatly resisted the truth when Copernicus proposed his theory of the earth's rotation around the sun. This is saying that our mental lumps are not always ready to yield when the truth comes. If we have built our house on one set of assumptions, we may not want to tear in and replace the sill after the house is almost finished. Hence the truth starts to be our enemy because the bigger it is, and the more faulty our foundation, the more emotional expense for replacement.

Instead of using our energies in search of more light and truth, we often turn to defending the falseness in our own structures. This can happen to us in every area of our personal, family, community, social, political, financial, or religious life.

Remember we are dealing with a child's mind first that comes to the wide wonderful world with all those questions of "what is it?" and "why is it?"

Where do lies start? It is understandable that the child gets new information and gives up storks and Santa Claus, but where does the truth become so painful that he refuses to go down that road any further? Where does denial of the truth become so important?

Is our belief about the truth more important than the truth? Will we defend that belief or interpretation rather than continuing our search for truth? Is loyalty to a person so great that one defends this person or his cause at the expense of truth? Are we afraid the truth will destroy us?

The fear of truth is a valid fear. Unless truth is set in relationship to love and grace it can be a destructive force. Truth might be likened to the sun. Warmth and light from the sun can heat and illuminate our houses. Gazing into the sun's rays can destroy our sight.

From our position at middle age, it is healthy to reexamine some of the basic questions that we asked as a four-year-old child. We need to realize how little we really know about the answers and how much we have accepted from our heritage that sounds like a "should" or an "ought." What is your origin? What values are worth spending the rest of your energy for? It is not weakness if you do not know. It is not wicked to be ignorant. It is unfortunate to continue to build on a foundation that is false.

There is yet another kind of lump in the mental life . . . it is the one where we take in the truth or truths of life without making them our own. Fritz Perls calls this an *introject,* meaning a thing that is not absorbed and assimilated. Perls says, "The food of facts and attitudes on which our personalities are built has to be assimilated in exactly the same way as our actual food." [1]

The swallowing whole of truth may be necessary because we may not have time to integrate it on the spot. Yet our lumps need, in time, to be digested, and made a part of us. A political leader might ask you to accept on trust that he is taking the right action. Later on you might learn facts from behind the scenes, facts he could not reveal at the time, to justify his actions. So you feel it was all right to swallow and chew later as cows do. We take these things in with the promise like Scarlet O'Hara, "I'll think about that tomorrow." In other words we take in a lot, or I should say, at middle age, we have taken in a lot. It may be time to think about it!

In conclusion, let us apply truth to these different areas.

The truth is, we don't get out of childhood without being so afraid of our feelings that we deny we have some of them. This is not a great fault in the child, because the child actually feels his survival is at stake, even though he is wrong in that assumption. At middle age, it is time to act on the truth that we *can* be accepted and loved with those lumps inside us. We can know that all other persons out there had the same sort of thing, and they are tired of dragging these lumps around. We need each other, and somebody has to take the risk of pulling the Sunday dress off some of these hidden feelings and letting them melt in the warmth of other people's acceptance.

The mind grows on truths that lead toward the Truth. We need some more truth every day if we are going to keep on growing; the more truth, the more growth. But our growth is not done alone, just as we do not get truth by ourselves for ourselves. It is for the community and sharing with others. It is a falsehood we tell ourselves that we must protect others from the truth we discover . . . it ceases to be truth. Neither can we grow if we defend ourselves from the truth others discover.

We may need to become as little children in the presence of truth because children keep on asking questions. We don't know much, we don't have many answers. Socrates went about Athens asking if any man had the truth, he confessed he didn't have it. He concluded his search with the conviction that man ought to be loving in the search for wisdom. In contrast Jesus taught that man ought to be wise in his loving: "Be wise like serpents and harmless like doves."

The truth for the body is, then, the same as for the mind—to be loving. Love dissolves our lumps of the emotional and mental life because it puts us in the right relationship to other humans.

If you have fought with people, nature, truth, and reality to get to middle age, OK. You are not by yourself. It is time now to ask if you want to keep on in the same struggle against the protest of body, in impaired circulation, or the mind, in its fears and uncertainties. Maybe it is time to consider whether you want to take a break from it all and become more wise in your loving.

9. Making Things Add Up

The world around us puts a "no-no" on craziness. The values we have at middle age say if you have a choice between being immoral or crazy, it is better to be immoral. Our society looks with less scorn on the prison than the mental hospital. I'm not judging that situation, just realizing it is there. The plea of insanity before the judge is a way of saying, "I don't want to claim responsibility for my actions." Society would rather have a criminal killer at large than an insane killer. The first will look for one enemy to shoot, the latter will shoot at random.

There is quite a difference between having some craziness and being crazy. I suppose we all have some craziness while I will, by no means, say we are all crazy. The difference here is quite important.

The Computer Symbol

The human mind is infinitely more complex than the most advanced computer, but let us use the computer as a sort of image for the moment. The mind takes all the experiences that come through the five senses, and it files these bits and pieces in something of the way a computer assembles data.

The mind of a child has quite a struggle to put things together, because the child doesn't have enough experience to absorb all that is pouring in. It takes experience to make sense out of experience. The frustrated father said to his son, "For me to tell you something, you've got to know something."

When an experience comes, it can quickly find a filing place in that part of the mind that is marked out for other experiences like it; it becomes just another one of those, only a little different perhaps. For example, a restaurant advertises its special new recipe for chicken; they say it is different from any other chicken you ever ate. You try it out, and it is different, but still the mind files the experience under the heading "chicken" with an extra tag on it for the uniqueness of flavor.

We try to economize in the mental process and not open new files unless this becomes absolutely necessary. The first time I ever ate bullfrog I tried to spare myself the bother of opening a new spot for it because it tasted a little like chicken, but also a bit like fish. Then perhaps it could be likened to turtle even more. Round and round I went, trying to get bullfrog under some subheading that would save working out a special and different place for it. As I came to eat more bullfrog, it became delicious enough in its own right that I can now say that it has its own place.

The story was told of a Louisiana Frenchman (the people we call Cajuns) that he was cleaning an armadillo, and was asked by a surprised passerby if he ate armadillo. The Frenchman replied that he did, and found them very good. The passerby asked what they tasted like, whereupon the Frenchman answered, "About like an owl."

The world outside is gradually becoming a world inside as we process the things we taste, see, hear, smell, and feel. A part of this processing is a mental activity of classifying all that we encounter, putting things that are alike together and deciding the measure of difference between things. Nature does not wear tags to tell you what plants go in the same "family" or genus; it is never like the botanical gardens. It was not until Aristotle that man learned to mentally economize by grouping animals or plants into categories of kinship. He seemed to be the first to see an order or system in nature itself. The ability to give order to nature is not in nature itself but in the human mind.

The problem for the child in assimilating experience comes in the fact that the child has not yet developed a method of classifying things. At first color is so important that anything red might be in a family with all other reds. This could include balls, toys, blouses, and kitchen curtains . . . all being red are all alike. Food could be divided into two categories, that which tastes pleasant and that which is unpleasant. Milk is not the same if it is too hot, too cold, or sour. To the infant it is "not-milk." Some babies even get a mother and a not-mother all in the same person, depending on whether she is loving or anxious, caring or preoccupied. So children are like primitive people who internalize the outside world with no system or principal of order. They take on one experience after another and get a mass of individual pieces scattered about, waiting for better ways to put them all in more comfortable relationship.

There are the lumps a child must take that are more serious than the day-to-day intake of ordinary things. For example, Mary Ben gave her childhood experience of the death of her little brother, along with the death of a whole family. The sorrow and wailing of her parents and grandparents was more than she could absorb, so this experience was much too powerful to relate to any other thing she ever felt. It had to be isolated in the computer for fear of overloading the circuits. It could only come out recently and start getting related to all other feelings and experiences.

I suppose the biggest lumps for children are based largely on, "Where did I come from and where am I going?" In order not to be too shocking about sex and death, we explain these mysteries with even greater ones, telling the child the stork brought him, and assure him about his destiny that the angels will carry him away. Our only consistency is that we guard the secret with feathers on both ends!

An early assumption of the child is one that the world moves by magic. This comes from the child's ability to control the family by making his wishes known. A cry gets action! The child keeps on using it as long as it gets results. Some persons never quite give it up as a last resort when everything else fails. The child within the adult is reluctant to give up all the magic. We can give it up in nearly every other area sooner than in religion, and it is there we sometimes hope God will move if we cry.

We may need to make some distinction between magic and miracle. For the time being let us say magic is an attempt to control a power you don't have, while miracle is the working of a power you don't understand. I want to give up my childhood craving for magic, but not my expectation of miracle. Someone might say that is a part of my craziness, and that's OK.

Oil in the Water

Let us add another symbol without giving up the one of the computer. The mind assimilates experience like a river taking the creeks and branches that drain as the river flows. The river takes each of these deposits of water and makes them its own, but these days it has a problem with pollution, sewage, filth, and industrial wastes. Our greatest plague down here in the lower Mississippi Valley is the oil spill when oil barges break up or crash into one another pouring thousands of barrels of oil into the river. The water can't break down the oil and make it part of the river; it remains a foreign substance and does not mix in the stream.

A thing like oil in the river happens to us when we experience things that we cannot relate to other experiences. I recall a big one. It was August in 1945; I was a part of the Army left in Europe after V-E Day and was somewhat enjoying the lull before being sent to the Far East. The orders were on the way and were expected any day. Then came the news over the Armed Forces Radio that the atomic bomb had been dropped on Hiroshima. I remember walking about the old Austrian hotel where we were quartered, trying to make some sense out of such a thing. There was no place to file that experience; there had never been anything like it, not only in the history of warfare but also in the history of the race. This was a brand-new thing, it was a lump of the first magnitude. Somehow I knew that this awful day spelled peace; at least the end of World War II. But I also knew as I walked outside and down Adolf Hitler Street (the Austrians had not yet taken those signs down and renamed the street!) that I was walking into a whole new world of terror. The bomb that became the *answer* for one war, at the same time became the *question* for all future wars.

My feelings were dazed, the bright sunlight seemed hazy and dim, the food that day lost its taste. I didn't want to take on any new experiences; I had had more than I could chew in one radio broadcast. Oil had been poured into my stream; I wondered if I could ever pull all this together and understand it.

To this day I have not understood that experience fully, nor do I expect to ever recall it without shuddering with horror. Frankly, I had to open a new file when the news struck, but I confess that it doesn't merge or mix well with anything else inside me.

Take the above example and add to that a number of things in the personal area that might give trouble. The more such things we carry that are unrelated or unrelatable to other things, the more energy it takes to hold them in our bulging files. It is possible that one would finally want to call a halt on moving forward in order to work through some of the lumps in the overload of the past.

It is possible to slow down or pull aside like a motorist who has a flat on the interstate highway. Some people at middle age might do just that, assuming that it is time to go aside and put things right by reflecting, cogitating, sorting, and assimilating. Yet I prefer to go back to the oil and water symbol to make a suggestion. It is a fact that the oil does not mix in the river and, if left there, will pollute the ocean. The boat that spills the oil is never equipped to pick up the oil. It is foolish and hazardous to try to skim it off with improvised rigs. There is equipment set up for the purpose of taking care of the problem.

We are not called on to work all of the lumps out by ourselves. There are others who can help us separate out what we can't manage. They are there to give us light when we can bear it, and warmth when we need it. In this process we are not fighting in a losing battle, we join the battle that is common to all. In this way we can carry the things we don't understand, the pieces of craziness, until either the light or warmth helps us manage a little better.

We might even go on then to change our symbol from "oil in the water" to "oil on troubled waters."

A Crazy Risk for Approval

A crazy thing is something that the mind can't sort out or the emotions can't dissolve. When it is a thing that I feel should be concealed from others, there is more trouble. A woman speaking only briefly with me said she didn't understand her own actions because she kept getting into one affair after another at middle age. She concluded there must be some evil and sinful thing in her makeup that kept driving her on to repeat that which brought her pain and misery. That was her attempt to explain what she couldn't understand and couldn't accept. She explained her dis-ease to herself as a piece of foreign material that kept on controlling her . . . as if "it" had a will of its own . . . "evil and sinful." Perhaps, to her, it seemed better to give it a bad name than not to name it at all because it is human to call a thing crazy if you can't name it. I remind you that in this present society it seems better to be immoral than insane.

The woman had come to me to avoid going back to her own pastor who had given her help a year before. Now she was ashamed to tell him she had slipped again. I thought it proper that she continue to deal with him because going from one to another in her counseling could be repeating the thing she deplored in the way she went from man to man with her emotions.

Our mental or emotional health is threatened when we divide up the inner life by forcing some part of ourselves into estrangement. Now I can't speak with much authority about the woman just mentioned, because I don't know her well enough. But I can speak with some knowledge of myself and others I know. We tend to identify the evil we feel as something that lives off our strength as a parasite that fell upon us from the outside. We want to disown it as if it were an illegitimate offspring.

Health is threatened when we get down on ourselves so that we punish ourselves for what we dislike inside us. We can never call ourselves OK when this occurs, but we depend on someone else to speak that word in loving care. Yet, we have to authorize them to speak it; we don't hear it unless we give them the right to speak.

You might easily allow or invite someone to give you just a touch of OK, perhaps enough to get you through the day. You allow them to lay a little on you, or to give you a stroke or two. As society sees it this is the reasonable thing to do.

There is a more "unreasonable" way to authorize the deeper affirmation of someone; that is, you trust and take the risk to lay your life open. The risk you run is that the other person will not hear you or be open to your need after you have exposed yourself. Not many people get wiped out when they take this risk, but the risk itself always makes you feel you are doing a daring and crazy thing. If the affirmation of OK-ness comes when you are exposed, you receive more than "daily bread," you get a whole year's harvest.

To be sure, we have need of the nibbles and morsels of approval, or OK, or "stroke" all through the day, every day. Some people need it more often than others. When I am speaking to a group of people, I pick out the "nodders" and look often in their direction for a show of agreement. They are as necessary to a good delivery as anything else for me. Recently I did a tape for a television program. I wrote what I thought was good material, but I quaked at the thought of speaking enthusiastically into a recording device. Then I hit upon an idea that saved the day. The camera man would be looking at me all the time, and I reasoned that if this material could turn him on, it might say something the next day when it was played to an audience. So I got him going with me, nodding and smiling. When the recording was over, I returned some of the strokes, telling him how he had helped bring it off.

Let me illustrate from another situation about our frequent need for approval. One day I caught the old streetcar in downtown New Orleans to ride home, about four miles distance. I sat just behind the conductor on the side opposite him. He caught my nod of approval as he screeched his brakes to keep from hitting a truck that dashed across the tracks. This was all he needed to know, he had a passenger who would help him. Each time there was a minor scrape he would look back for another nod of approval. The approval sought was that he was an OK guy with a miserable job having to deal with so many crazy people along the tracks. I hadn't realized how many tangles a streetcar could have in seventy blocks and each tangle called for another stroke! By the time I got off the streetcar I was depleted and exhausted; I had no power left, because I had been giving and not getting. In making my exit from the car, I made a resolve never to ride with that conductor again and if fate should put me on his run, I would sit all the way in the rear! He was so hungry for strokes, he should have been the conductor of a streetcar called "Desire."

The conductor who took nibbles every few seconds was

in need of a lot of approval; so was the woman who wanted to deal with her "evil and sinful" ways. The woman was driving herself into some craziness over her behavior, and the conductor was driving others out of their wits in the way he took from them without authorization. We will deal next with how we spend our emotions.

Feelings Get Confused

My own loss of power in the streetcar ride was that I allowed the conductor to take from me what I really didn't want to give: namely a nod or a smile at least once every two blocks, sort of agreeing with him that there were a lot of stupid people he was having to put up with, either the bad and reckless drivers or the bold and daring pedestrians. He conned me into a passive agreement that he was the good guy while all those others were bad people he had to endure. It was a game with myself, the game of telling myself I could "feed the hungry," and allow the hungry to be in control of how much they took.

I choose now not to play that game and not to allow another to pull my string and cut it off where he chooses. I will be in charge of saying when it is to be cut. Neither will I avoid the conductor by sitting in the rear; if I do that, he still has the power. I will sit where I sat, but I will find a way next time to provide a chance for him to give me something in exchange for what I give him. It would be good for him to learn that he can give to his passengers as well as take away from them.

There are many occasions where we get depleted in pouring out strokes "you're OK" without noticing that none are coming in. We look upon our reserves as an endless string that others can pull and cut at will, as if we would never be fully unraveled. But it does happen to us; we run low of potency or power in much the same way a free spender runs out of cash. It leaves us depleted, and you know the next step in the game.

After you run dry in giving where you didn't want to give, you can turn next to take from people who don't want to give to you. So having allowed ourselves to be emptied in an unreal game, we seek to fill ourselves up again by changing the scene and making a raid on an unsuspecting wife, friend, or employee. In the game, we get "down," or show we are down, to one who is up so that we can drain off their power for ourselves. The confusion only increases until somebody has the will and courage to call a halt to such games and demand that the stealing stop.

In order to clear up some of the craziness and confusion, we can deal with our emotions as honestly as we deal with our money. Our computer keeps all the data, it knows where we have borrowed or overspent. Other people have their computers running, keeping the same kind of records. The following situations might compare emotions with money.

Money and Emotions

There are emotional *beggars* who work on pity. They want you to look down on them and toss a coin in their cup. You feel bad if you do or if you don't.

— — —

There are emotional *thieves* who steal from you in a weak moment. They disarm you with a grief they do not have, to get from you what you would not otherwise give.

— — —

There are emotional *free spenders* who pour out lavish

praise. When you try to give them something back, they tell you to keep the change.

_ _ _

There are emotional *borrowers* who take from you what you have on the promise that tomorrow they will pay you back.

_ _ _

There are emotional *loan sharks* who give to you, but make you pay double for everything you get from them.

_ _ _

There are emotional *blackmailers* who demand, by threatening to expose you for some emotional dishonesty along the way. They keep the best set of records! For example, I knew a professional person who used people's confidences to extort gifts from them.

_ _ _

Now to briefly elaborate on these various characters just pictured. The emotional beggar is not usually seen in the social class of beggars. He passes with every mark of respectability in outward appearances. Yet, he is the person who gets his strokes by having other people feel sorry for him; he puts himself down in order to get others to lift him up by telling him he is not as bad as all that. He always gives the pessimistic side of the doctor's report about his health, and he lets old scars from the past show. He puts himself in the victim role and hooks those who have a need to rescue him from his miseries. He convinces others that all the breaks went against him or that he was framed or plotted against or that he was passed over for a deserved promotion. With such a line he draws pity, and in getting it, he not only feels bad about it, he also makes those feel bad who give it. He leaves the party with all these banked-up bad feelings and must afterward avoid the people whom he drained because he is so in debt to them, he would rather not face them again. This makes him feel even worse, so he goes out seeking more and more pity without being able to put things right in this game.

The emotional thief is not a bank robber, or a cheat at cards, he just happens to be dishonest about what he feels. He gives out a false report. He shouts, "Wolf, wolf!" when there is no wolf. He seeks to cash in on the kind of sympathy people draw for their support when they have a great loss. He holds on to a past loss longer than is proper because it still stirs people's sympathy when he repeats it with a tear or two. He puts himself in the bind that he gets no support when a real sorrow comes his way because he has already overdrawn his account in that particular bank with his friends.

The emotional free spender has already been illustrated as the one who assumes he has strokes for everybody on every occasion, while he assumes he does not need anyone to affirm *him*. At all cost he keeps up the facade that he can cheer up the fainthearted and make the weary happy again. He does it, not with a real optimism based on hope, but rather with a more boisterous backslapping ritual. He never stops to question that his own feelings may be depressed. He gets into the positive thinking frame and tries to rationalize people out of their bad feelings. He tells them why they have no reason for being down, hence he makes them feel guilty for being the way they are. So they take on his seeming gaity as an act to keep from being put down, while they resolve to avoid him the next time they get into trouble.

The emotional borrower is one who has run out of

resources but is too proud to admit that he needs someone to give him a lift. He doesn't realize that there are a lot of people who need to be needed, and that these same people would be glad to meet his needs. He must keep his needs concealed and not let anyone know he, of all people, would ever resort to knocking, seeking, or asking. He only wants a little touch; tomorrow he will have more than enough. With that attitude he discounts his need, therefore the person who gives to him is deprived of the chance to be of meaningful help. The borrower assumes it is a weakness to ever have need of others. He is ashamed to cry over a loss that hurts, and if someone offers a hand or a shoulder, he is ever so careful to belittle himself over whatever he receives and promises he will overcome this weakness forthwith.

The emotional loan shark is the one who takes advantage of those who are in some kind of acute need without the normal support of friends. He offers to be a "friend in need," but he is not a friend. He is an opportunist. In exchange for the support he gives in a crisis, he lays claim on the loyalty and support later for a few crumbs given to the hungry.

The emotional blackmailer poses as the dispenser of wisdom and mercy so that the one he offers to help is misled into revealing his weakness or his need. The blackmailer may go to the trouble to actually help and draw the affection of the one he helped. The blackmailer collects these he has helped into a little colony of supporters so that they organize to carry out his wishes and desires all the while believing they are working for the humanitarian cause.

You tend to handle your emotions about like you handle your money. In being honest with yourself, you might improve the way you spend and withhold. It is OK also if you discover a little craziness in either of these areas.

Fantasy, Ecstasy, and Preoccupation

We have already said that a human being takes the exterior world of nature (and society) and digests it so that what is outside us is reflected inside us. None of us has a perfect mirror or a complete understanding so that the world we see is always the one that is. Our growth depends on constantly changing and correcting what we once held as an answer, as we get better answers.

Sometimes we just get weary of trying to cope with the world we have. We use one of the uncanny powers at our disposal to make another world, one of our own choosing and delight. That is the power of fantasy, and I suppose we have all used it to make a dozen or so worlds of our own. For example, if we are having a tough time paying our bills, we might escape to a place where money grows on trees or where rich uncles bestow their savings on us. If we are frustrated in love, we can sing a ballad of imaginary victory; if we feel pains from going without acclaim, we create a world where all the others look up to us, seek our advice, or invite us to their party.

Everybody has the craziness of a little fantasy. We all need some rest from the real world when it gets too heavy for us to manage. Perhaps it gets too painful in shutting doors of opportunity, or it topples what we have built, or it deprives us of someone we love.

We may turn to fantasy in order to recover what we feel we have lost. Fantasy is a little lie we tell ourselves to hold some of the pain back, pain that may be more than we can manage at the time. Yet, in our fantasy, we don't even see the pain, that is the purpose of the fantasy—

to take the pain out.

Some people get upset that they are caught in their fantasies more than they like; they fear that this is unhealthy and a show of instability. The unhealthy fantasy is the one we indulge in so freely or fully that it finally comes and takes us away when it pleases, and brings us back only when it chooses. This degree of fantasy is serious and calls on us to get back in charge wherever it was we left our mental life unguarded. If we can't look at the truth of the pain or the truth of reality, we may need someone to help us with it. Sometimes it takes a professional.

Too much fantasy says we have cut people out in order to amuse ourselves, and to relate to fictional characters, our own brainchildren. If it goes that far, we need to realize we have chosen the unreal over the real. We also need to remember that reality, though more painful, is infinitely more rewarding than fantasy. The characters of fantasy can never give us the blood warmth of an embrace. If we get a friend or a professional counselor to help us with fantasy, we can best use them to help us make the choice of putting reality first. Nobody can make that choice for us, nor can they make it easy. Only the person knows what it takes to put such overindulgence to an end.

Fantasy is an unreal attempt to chew up and digest the past lumps that linger unsolved. But it makes two errors in that it tries to chew without teeth, and it denies that the lumps are a threat by turning them into something painless or harmless. It reflects everything in our own looking-glass world, and from there we may see pain as pleasure or darkness as light. Maybe this is why people can get high on fantasy and prefer to stay in it or to return often to it.

Earlier we spoke of ecstasy as an experience of standing outside; we are not calling fantasy the same sort of thing. Ecstasy is the joy of seeing our reality and being happy about it, while fantasy is creating a substitute reality and enjoying our own act of creation. Fantasy holds a dread that it must finally burst like a bubble, while ecstasy leaves its glow on things like the sparkle of the early morning dew even after it is gone.

Fantasy can be compared with preoccupation, yet they are different. Preoccupation is a mix of either the past lump or some future anxiety related to the present. It is an attempt to give our attention in two directions without a real focus anywhere. For example, a person is carrying on a conversation with his friends while he is wondering if his last job interview is going to bring results. Neither subject gets his full attention, and not much gets done in the conversation or the worrying. Preoccupation is more nearly compared to a worry or a concern over real issues, but its method is usually unfruitful. Preoccupation is something we all do at times; it also is a little craziness.

In conclusion, I would like to illustrate from our experiences as a couple. Mary Ben is not nearly so afraid of her craziness as I am; in fact she worries me at times that she can be almost completely free to be herself, no matter how others around her might feel. For example, she will pick up a piece of what seems junk to me, or a rock when there's no room in the car, or a piece of weathered pine board. Five years later she will assemble the pieces and out comes something unbelievably beautiful and original.

This is a sort of symbol of how the pieces of the past can finally add up to meaning and growth, pieces that seemed to have no place until some occasion comes where we can use them.

10. Getting and Giving Blessing

From the time I was about six years old, I began to notice two things going on in my family. First, my grandfather seemed cold toward my father, the oldest of five sons and one daughter. At the same time he was always delighted to be around his second son in a special way. There was sparkle in his eye when Benny walked in, while he didn't pay attention to my father's presence or his conversation. Since the family was rural and deep south, it was very much a patriarchy. The second thing I noted with painful feelings was the fact that my father (with three sons) gave his attention and affection to son number two, Eldred. My oldest brother and I felt at times by Eldred like the sons of Jacob felt toward Joseph with his coat of many colors. It all focused on the fact that our father's eye showed a special joy in his blessed son. We were shut out of that closeness that they shared. It never occurred to me that my father and grandfather were living out the same pattern by showing marked partiality to son number two.

The memory awakened and made sense some forty years later as I summed up a number of cases in personal counseling. Over and over I kept running into these patterns of partiality. These are some things I noted with frequency:

The father tends to be partial to (and bless) his second

son and his first daughter.

The mother tends to be partial to (and to bless) her first son and her second daughter.

All other things being equal, the most blessed child will spring farthest out from home.

The more unblessed children tend to work hard for approval.

The more blessed children expect approval to come from everywhere. This expectation has a lot to do with bringing blessing into being.

Don't put this down as a rigid law, because I have observed many variations. Usually where the pattern is different, there are some very unusual circumstances. For example, a woman with five sons blessed her second, as did her husband. She was so in need of blessing from her husband that she blessed the child of his choice in order to get the husband's affirmation. There are a thousand different such things that can interrupt the typical pattern.

A Middle-Aged Look at Blessing

Maybe you say your parents loved all of their children alike; that there was never any show of partiality or favoritism. If that is the way it was, you don't need to read this chapter; it is written for those who know all the children were not the same in their parent's eyes.

The blessing is often the focus of unfinished business between us and parents at middle age. My father remained bound all his days and could never pull himself away from his poor farm life nestled up against my grandfather's home. Yet, I don't think he ever knew what it was he hungered so much to get. He never had a word for it. My father had my grandmother's blessing, but in a patriarchal structure, that was no match for the father's blessing. Things are different in the social order today regarding a woman's blessing.

If you didn't get the blessing from your mother or father, it is time to deal with the pain and grief of it in order to get on with your life. It can be the grief of your life. Here are some observations you might consider.

Blessed children don't get caught so much in guilty feelings that drive them to do for parents things they otherwise resist.

Blessed children have their own lives apart from their parents . . . they have their own friends.

Blessed children give and receive from parents without as much obligation.

Blessed children can celebrate with their parents . . . or apart from them.

Blessed children can accept the aging of their parents.

Blessed children can more easily accept their parent's death, when it comes.

These are only rough guidelines; there are many others.

The unblessed tend not to believe that they can be loved and accepted just as they are. They didn't get acceptance from parents, and may be scripted to be untrusting that it can come from any other place. They are usually hard workers for approval, and take their strokes from their doings. They don't tend to feel good about themselves. In contrast, the blessed feel OK about who they are. They had somebody to sparkle on them as children, and they tend to keep on sparkling and striking sparks most everywhere they go.

Usually we use *blessed* to talk about good people and *unblessed* to describe bad ones. Not so! The blessed are very often like Jacob, the arrogant, the unthinking, the proud. Actually the unblessed elder brother, in the parable of the prodigal son, is the good son. He stays home, tends the farm, goes to his church, raises a family, and keeps on hoping he will make it one day with his father. He is the kind of person we all want for a neighbor. We can count on him to keep his grass cut, his hedges trimmed, and his house painted.

I'm saying it is OK if you didn't get a parental blessing. Maybe I'm saying it because I never got it from my father. To be sure, I went back many times to the old well before finally admitting it was dry. That spells grief because we hope to get all we need for life from the parental source, enough to run us for as long as we live. But if it is not there, it is not there, period.

We need to go through the grief in order that we might authorize a new source of blessing. If we don't give it up, we can stay blocked up, preventing the word of OK from anyone from reaching our person. Here is an example:

I was sharing the blessing concept with a group of some twenty people. One lady of middle years told how she hurt because her father didn't turn on and sparkle for her. She had done all she knew, but kept trying, with no good results. He was ill now and might die; she was terrified at the prospect of losing him unless he changed. I knew she couldn't let anyone else bless her until she finished her business with her father. In order to test these feelings, I surprised her with the questions, "Would you let me bring you the blessing?" She drew back quickly and said, "Not yet!" This same story could be repeated several times.

You cannot be blessed by someone you don't authorize. If you authorize someone who doesn't or can't bless you, I have to ask you if you are not actually choosing to stay unblessed. In this way you can return to the old familiar bad feelings and feel sorry for yourself.

Turn the whole matter around: if you got parental blessing, then it is not enough to take you the remainder of your journey. The child inside you will never cease to delight in the blessing of parents. The adult in you needs a different affirmation . . . the affirmation of a peer or peers.

If you got the blessing of parents, you need to give that up now in order to be centered in the adult world. If you didn't get it, you need to do the same and give it up in order to move forward emotionally as an adult.

Toward a Definition of Blessing

By this time some of you will be annoyed at the concept of blessing. I can't really define it any more than you can define love. Yet, the following might help some.

Go back to ancient and primitive times when Abraham blessed Isaac. It was a sort of deathbed scene where Abraham passed along, as it were, his life to his son. He gave him his sexual potency, his cattle and herds, his fields and flocks. He gave all that he was and all that he had; he blessed Isaac.

In even more primitive experience, with the practice of cannibalism, the patriarch or tribal chief was sometimes eaten in old age that the males of the tribe might get his blessing. This could add some powerful meaning to "Take, eat, this is my body"—in doing this you get the blessing, you get the potency or power of the Christ. This is the way he transmits it. Note the difference between Abraham's gift of blessing to only one and the apostle Paul saying that Abraham's blessing is given by Jesus to the many.

Take another example, John the Baptist. John was a

most powerful person; his power grew every time he refused to be named as the Messiah. He fit into all of the
patterns of Jewish expectation, yet he refused. He saved
up all that power and transmitted it to Jesus in public
at the baptism, telling the nation that he, John, was not
the one they looked for, but rather Jesus, an unknown
name from the village of Nazareth. Having emptied his
vessel of power on Jesus, you could say John blessed Jesus.
He had no more power after that act. It was like a candidate
bowing out of a race. Once you bow out and transfer your
power to someone else, it is gone.

What John did was name his candidate with no more
privilege of making another nomination. Later he had
second thoughts, but not a second chance. Hence Jesus
said there was none born among women greater than John.
Usually John's kind of giving the self is saved for a son
or a daughter or at least someone close in the family. John
only blessed once, or specially; perhaps Jesus took all that
potency and strength that John gave and worked out the
way to bless more than one.

Blessing has two sides: one might be called the *authority*
blessing, that which is given from father to son, or that
which is given in a very limited or special way. The other
is the *peer* blessing; it goes out, not down.

The child inside us will keep on reaching out for an
authority blessing and that is OK. We play the game of
giving authority persons some kind of special magic they
don't have just to keep us in touch with our childhood
past. The authorities take the place of big daddies or big
mammas; they look after the world if we want to go out
and play.

The adult inside us wants to claim that being human
is OK; that it is more important to be human than to

be an "authority," that the gift of humanity is greater than all of the magic. The adult wants to touch and be touched by life at the center, by sharing and giving, and loving and caring. Such adult-to-adult relationship can be peer blessing. It is not ever easy for parents and children to be adults to each other in an open and free manner. It does happen occasionally, but it is important not to get hung up trying to make something work that doesn't often work. Can you let it be if you can't be friends with your mother or father? Some of the problems might come from their side. Getting freed up here will give you more ease to move closer to others who are peers where you both give and receive blessing.

Blessing and Curse

Blessing is perhaps better understood in contrast to curse.

Curse is the attempt to get hold of the childhood wish for power and magic in order to do harm to someone, to speak damnation on them, or to register a fierce disapproval.

Primitive religion operated with the power to curse: it threatened with death and destruction in order to control people's impulses. Even the teachings of Moses were: Don't do it lest you die. The child inside us still feels the threat of curse as being much of the power of religion.

Within our feelings, we tend to give more power to the curse than to the blessing; it is as if the destructive forces outmatched the creative energies. This may be true on the politico-scientific scene, but does it have to be so in the religioemotional area?

I'm daring to suggest that blessing has greater power than curse. In fact, the blessing in all its potency leaves you with less need to go back to the magic in order to curse. Yet, this is not saying that blessing is a touch of magic that rubs off on metals and prayer shawls, a magic that is balanced against voodoo and witchcraft, or one used to fight them off.

The feeling of curse is not a strange thing in the family. Some fathers and mothers let it be known that whoever goes against tradition gets the curse, such as is given by the godfather. It is never easy for son or daughter to buck the parental curse, which may only be a show of disapproval or a refusal to give approval.

The wedding scene is the place we understand parental blessing or curse. The question arises with the offspring whether their choice of a mate is going to be OK with parents. Sometimes children never get the OK, or the blessing. The blessing of the church represents God and community, which is hopefully added to parental blessing or is used to offset parental "curse" or failure to approve.

The Reversal of Blessing

Sometimes we get things upside down regarding the blessing. An example is an unblessed person who places his hopes in son or daughter who will go out in the big world and "make a name" or bring a blessing on the father's name. I have talked to a couple of young Roman Catholic priests, who at ordination found it extremely difficult to carry the ritual to completion and bless their fathers. One said he had great difficulty in getting his hands up to place them on his father's head. This was a father who had never blessed his son.

An immigrant father bases his hope for acceptance in an alien culture on his son. He denies himself the satisfaction of more education in order to educate his son. He then looks to that son to be his blessing. That son usually doesn't know what's going on, but his second nature resists blessing the father . . . at least he resists being the first to bless. His feelings say he wants the father's blessing that he might be enabled to return the blessing.

A part of the mix-up at middle age is the need to bless or be a blessing to parents when our feelings hunger for their blessing first so things can move in their proper order. There is an awkwardness or shyness or embarrassment in a son or daughter initiating the blessing toward parents. We just have the natural knowledge that water runs down hill. If we are going to reach "up" and bless, we somehow can't do it well. We often take bad feelings from the attempt to bless parents if it is before we have received from them. Our own child of the past doesn't want to see the hunger and nakedness of our parents. We want to keep alive the fiction that they are a well that never runs dry.

The Blessing and Your Children

Turn and look the other way for a change, at least with a promise that you are going to finish some things with your parents. How is it between you and your children? Are they all blessed? Have you done enough to make them secure in the knowledge that you accept them as persons of worth just as they are?

Maybe you show partiality, perhaps one child gives you special delight, or you can talk with one and not the other. Maybe, like my father, you did what your father did, in about the same way. Yet, you have learned that "all men are created equal," and you want to uphold that as a truth for you and your family. You detest the inequality of favoritism, so you set about to discipline your feelings for getting out of line with the Constitution of the United

States. Thomas Jefferson must be right, we tell ourselves, and with this assumption we put ourselves down.

It is true that two brothers are "equal before the law," but they are not necessarily equal in parental affection. The law tries to even up the mountains and valleys created by the convulsive and fitful spasms of partial love.

Your children can hook your guilt by hinting that you are partial to another sibling. You will up the allowance to stop such talk! You are even more threatened when the neighbors notice these differences in the way you feel by your children, or act by them.

Taking these things of partiality and inequality into your feelings, what will you do to put it right? What can you do, spend the rest of your life trying to undo what you did? There is no way you can ever square off with that part of your past. One child might say your debt is for all time, and they would have you busy paying the installments.

The fact of partiality in your past or present is really your business. There isn't one human alive and no law on the books that can regulate how you love or don't love. The law can regulate how you give (in your will) but not how you love. Some give more things to unblessed children to even the score about giving the feelings to another. That will also keep the neighbors confused!

You could be one of those parents who never got blessing from your own parents, so you turn to your child or children to get it. This often comes out of the assumption that blessing ought to spring from the family, not outsiders. If you bought that assumption, maybe you need to take a hard second look. Blessing can come from whatever source you authorize. This is saying I can't authorize myself, nor can any third person authorize me to bless you.

That can come from you alone. Someone can come to you as the world's number one giver of blessing, yet they can do nothing for you unless you give the nod that you are willing to receive it.

Your children never earn your blessing even though they may think earning is the way to get it. Perhaps you have a son or daughter who has labored long and faithfully to get your sparkle and you don't have it for them. If you don't have it, you can't fake it, can you? Don't they need release to go find it for themselves? Will your guilt allow you to send a child forth in an unfinished state of blessing? Is it all right that a son or a daughter might find blessing somewhere else?

Some children cash in on our need to bless by not receiving what we want to give. How can I look powerful if they don't take the good stuff I offer and make use of it? Remember also that a blessing you need to give is not a blessing, it may be a control. The child who refuses to take what you need to give wins out in the game of getting control.

If you are free to bless, you may be free not to bless, or to accept that, in some situations, things are not OK for the blessing to take place. If you bless out of obligation, you only half bless. You can't give what you don't have, and it is lost effort to "bless" for the sake of appearances. If you risk being real with your children, they may one day turn that into a blessing.

Only the Truth Blesses

We often think of the deathbed scene as the blessing, that thing you have to say when you have only enough breath to utter one sentence. When I was a child, my mother took turns with other women in the community to attend the sick and dying. We children were always concerned to have her tell us the "last words." To whom were the words spoken? What were the feelings? It was here we assumed a dying person would shake off all the masks and speak the truth. Whatever they said should be heeded as a guide to the living.

I have long since learned that the dying are not concerned to take off their masks. If they have carried the pretense this far, they want support to play the game out to the end. Approaching death doesn't as often make people honest as it makes them frightened. They more often seek a blessing than they seek to give blessing. Their feelings respond sometimes to death as the curse that has more power than the promise of the blessing to make all things new. Hence our greatest truth doesn't come from sickbeds, though some of it might. Perhaps our truth should be given to the sick to support them in their deepest fears and uncertainties. It could be a sick faith that built its case on the experiences of sick people, or a dying faith that got its support from visions of dying people.

At middle age we have opportunity to decide if we will keep on wearing the masks. Some of us are weary of our games and pretenses that run both ways; in one direction to our parents, in another direction to our children. Blessing is the power to separate the generations (as the doctor cuts the umbilical cord to give an infant life apart from its mother).

The truth is: blessing to yourself is that power that makes you free from whatever cords cling from the generations—the power that allows you to make a claim in your own right rather than earn it from another source.

11. To Women Only

A syndrome of middle age is the realization that the future is not forever. We are beginning to feel the deadline to get our act together. It's time to take a look at ourselves—to claim the knowledge in our mind and feelings that the life we hold is housed in this mind-body-spirit that we call "I."

At this point, health is a major consideration. The way our body functions, the way our mind works, and the attitude that we have toward the future all determine our state of health.

The World Health Organization of the United Nations defines health as "a state of complete physical, mental and social well-being, and not merely the absence of disease and infirmity." [1]

One of the first physical symptoms of middle age is a little farsightedness. Your reading material needs to move away a little. To correct this problem, I bought a pair of magnifying glasses at the five-and-dime store. They were great!

I returned and got a pair for Myron. I knew I could suit him. We see eye to eye!

Myron went to the optometrist.

The doctor tested his eyes. As an honest friend he said, "You can take this prescription and have some reading glasses made up. Or you can wear the ones that Mary Ben got for you. They'll do just as well."

Almost every book that deals with middle-age health comments on whether men experience menopause. I'm only prepared to say from my experience that they certainly do not go through the dramatic involution that women undergo. Women's experiences are almost as different as the lives that they bring to middle age. Their attitude, background, number of children, sex experiences all play part in the drama of body change of this time.

Some women need to be separated from the physical apparatus of childbearing. It has served its purpose but continues to drain strength and vitality. Modern surgical procedure has made the hysterectomy a relatively safe operation. Others are fortunate that nature has been gracious enough to spare them surgery. A wonderful bonus of our time is that medicine enables women to get through menopause with a minimum of discomfort. New drugs help control symptoms that range all the way from severe mental anguish to great physical discomfort.

While we experience body change, the challenge is to accept the gift of the future and enjoy it in more comfort.

A special health consideration of women is our tendency to put on and keep unnecessary weight.

Statistics show that ten women to every one man is overweight. Nature laid it on us heavy. In my case, maintaining a slim body was a struggle after our family began to arrive. Mealtime, good food, and fun seemed to go together. At checkup time the doctor usually remarked, "You need to lose a few pounds!" At middle age I made the decision to claim information that I'd had all along. From under my stack of cookbooks, the matching set of diet books was pulled out. I lost about twenty pounds.

Practical application of ideas is a personal matter and each person must claim her own information about dieting. My remarks will be limited to my personal experience.

I started my diet by fasting two days. I drank a glass of water every hour on the hour to cleanse, circulate, and purify my body. This helps abate and control the appetite. Ladies react in different ways to dieting and fasting. It is a very personal experience and a time to get in touch with what the body is feeling and experiencing. Body and mind work together, but the spirit coordinates the process. I remember as a child hearing a plump friend tell my mother, "I went on this diet and at a committee meeting I got into a terrible argument with the chairperson. I realized that it was the diet that had made me get into this frame of mind. If this is what a diet does to me, I'll stay fat!"

And so she did. There are many arguments that we can get into with ourselves that sabotage our efforts for change. Altering our concept of ourselves takes willful courage whether it is a physical, mental, or spiritual venture.

Dr. Serino in *Reducing After Forty* acquainted me with why a person can diet a week and show a weight gain.[2] He stated that our water table gets out of balance. Water fills our cells and holds the place even after we've dieted and the fat is gone. Our cells are struggling with the hope that we'll nourish them again with the fat that they have grown accustomed to. After two weeks the cells give up, release the water, and shrink. The scales finally show our reward—by several pounds of weight loss.

The diet that worked for me was a protein-only diet, with just a nip of wild honey now and then. Remember the Scriptures tell us that John the Baptist lived on a diet of locusts (protein) and wild honey. It's an old diet.

I walked two miles a day—a regular routine for me. In the last year that exercise has taken on a whole new pleasure. Our daughter, Julie, has a new baby, William Myron, and lives just a mile from our home. The walking aids circulation and speeds the reaction of the weight-loss process.

I borrow an idea from Dr. Joyce Brothers. She states that the best beauty aids in life are free: diet, exercise, the right kind of sleep, clean skin, and most importantly—smile! [3]

Having a thinner more youthful image is reward indeed!

I even gave myself another reward. I did something that I've held as an idea for several years. I made and embroidered a really nice pantsuit and skirt—two sizes smaller than before.

It is a refreshing challenge to realize that women can change emphasis after their children are on their own. One couple said, "It's great to be back together again after all these years!"

We admit change: we have traded our youth for experience. Would you seriously want to go through any part of your life again?

The challenge is to accept the gift of the future as an opportunity for enjoying life! Women are the only part of the female creation who lives beyond her reproductive years. The quality of life is what we choose.

Our body goes through metamorphosis. We are new creatures!

Identify with the butterfly. Cultivate the spirit of joy!

Middle age can be the time of your life!

SECTION IV
MATE—
CHECKMATE

12. A Game? A Game!

In the sixties, those who held dear the tradition that love, marriage, and sex were a sacred trinity and to be experienced in that order received some real shock. Our generation was modeling the heritage that women married, had a family, loved their children, and kept the home. Fathers worked at their jobs, supported the family. We reacted to our responsibility in the "natural" way. Children of the sixties were not necessarily following that good example.

We became aware of some new information related to behavior and were interested in it, but knew that it did not apply to us, then began to wonder, does it?

Some of my best friends and teachers have been books that helped interpret relationship. I have claimed Missildine's *Your Inner Conflicts,* and more recently, *Born to Win* by Muriel James and Dorothy Jongeward for looking at my own experience. These books helped me begin thinking in terms of my relationships with others. They gave me some mental tools to work with.

On one occasion, Dr. Ken Pepper, a friend, was visiting and he, Myron, and I were discussing some of the new concepts of relationships that have come from transactional analysis his specialty. To make specific a generalization he said, "You see, Mary Ben, it's in Myron's best interest

for you to remain as you are in relation to that position."
"Aha!"
That set off a whole process of putting data through
my mental computer. Without being aware of it, Myron
and I were into some games.

The Garbage Game

I'll illustrate with a problem that I observe to be common
to the usual family—the handling and disposing of garbage.
This can be an emotion-charged transaction. It was one
of our family games.

When we moved to New Orleans, there were certain
rules and regulations laid on us by the sanitation department. Certain days were garbage days. Alternating days
were trash days. Myron read all the rules regarding texture,
height, weight, shape, size, wet, dry, bio-degradable and
non. He explained to the family.

When the boys put the garbage out—great!
When I put the garbage out—fine!
When Myron put the garbage out, we got an enormous
charge of anger. He reconciled his lecture to us, followed
by threats of no service, fines, arrest, jail!

"You won't learn the rules! You rise above all this like
it is not important!"

When I ventured that I have a happy, ongoing relationship with the garbagemen, he groaned, "Those poor
men!"

With some insight we realized that we had taken a
familiar situation and were reacting to it in a pattern of
behavior that felt "natural" to us. He was getting rid of
stored up feelings of anger, frustration. I reacted out of
my childhood when my father scolded me.

Two good things happened. Number one: Myron realized that he did not have to keep trying to teach me to sort out and classify the garbage. I was free to rise above the regulations and learn from authority rather than him (as I related). Number two: The sanitation department changed the rules.

The Guessing Game

In our culture some attitudes are taken for granted, "understood." Custom dictates that a woman does not come on too direct about some things. For example, in the early days of our marriage I understood that the wife was too aggressive if she made sexual desire known. Being coquettish and flirtatious was permitted as a part of the script but to take initiative in sexual matters was felt to be downright "trashy." I can't help noticing that passivity is not now in vogue. Young people have set an example of bringing issues out into the open and discussing them. The game of hidden feelings and indirect approach has been voted down in favor of honesty and frankness.

However, there needs to be the happy mix of subtlety and mystery coupled with openness and frankness in this, more than in most relationships.

Trying to figure out what is on a mate's mind can be a heavyweight problem in a marriage. Giving hints but not stating the problem is one way to get into that game. Trying to control without coming on straight and honest discounts the personal relationship with the mate as an equal adult partner. Sometimes directly stating "I would like for you to tell me exactly what is on your mind" can clear the air and start discussion. This recognizes the mate as a person—and states that there is a problem to be dealt with. "I know you'd like a fur coat for Christmas, so can we talk about that since I don't trust my judgment?" recognizes the problem and also calls for a meeting of minds. One of the motels advertises "the best surprise is no surprise." Sometimes the best surprise turns out to be disappointment when communication is lacking.

Marriage can bog down to passivity when one person assumes the right to think for the marriage partner. Have you ever had your mate volunteer you for a day of charity work for a really good cause? Being helping persons, Myron and I got into that early in our marriage. We made some decisions that we would talk that kind of situation over before we made that presumption again.

Working to make the home a partnership takes time and understanding on the part of each person in the family. Assuming that "good ol' mom" enjoys her traditional role doesn't necessarily make it so. Mom has a right to "claim her power" at this point and make her wishes felt.

Blame Game

Another game that we have recognized is the "Blame Game." When something goes wrong, it is necessary to fix the blame and see that punishment in the form of bad feelings, guilt, and hurt are experienced. The wrongdoer should be sorry for his deed. Air Force Chaplain Newt Cole comments: "Things have to get worse before they can get better." We justify this game in the name of teaching character and responsibility. A hard game of blame can get into the game of "court." I'll illustrate.

The family security is like our feelings toward the welfare of society.

The players are: offender, detective, police, attorney for defense, prosecuting attorney, judge.

The same person may serve in several different roles.

The electric iron left on all day will do as an example.

The peace has been breached!

The detective in the family gets out the Sherlock Holmes hat and deducts "Who is the culprit?" Mother may determine "Who left on the iron?" as police haul the offender into court. Court is ruled over by the judge—played by father or mother (who has just been acting as police and detective). Attorney for defense may be allowed to speak; that is, excuses may be made. The offender usually takes this privilege. The judge sternly delivers a lecture. In this court it is necessary to fix blame and make sure that shame is experienced.

As we think of communicating in the honesty of the moment, we try to keep issues in focus and discuss the problem at hand. In this way the integrity of the person is not threatened. As a child, I recall my sadness over the loss of a family pet for whose care I was responsible. My hurt was compounded by family blame and anger. This left me feeling not only sad, but stupid and unworthy as well.

Honestly dealing with issues and facing facts can result in a learning experience. As I so often heard the schoolchildren say to each other when they wanted teasing to stop, "I ain't playin'!" That stops the game. One way to realize that a game is going on is experiencing bad feelings from the exchange in relationship.

Myron has referred to the fact that he sat on his temper. This emboldens me to say that one of the healthy things in recent years is that we are giving ourselves permission to fuss. Several years ago I expressed to him that I felt deprived because we didn't have hassles. Our pattern was: one of us fussed, the other retreated, the first one felt guilty. In my parents' home hostile feelings built up. My father let out his anger in rage. For the most part Mother guarded

her feelings or expressed them to me. I had hoped we
would manage better.

Since we grew up in the same town, the virtues and
eccentricities of each set of parents are well known to us.
We can recognize and call them by name in ourselves
and in our children. It was not until our middle years
when we really delved into our parental backgrounds that
we gained new insight about how our parenting had affected our marriage. My need for emotional and financial
security made me anxious in ways that threatened Myron's
need for privacy and acceptance. In earlier years the condi-
tioning from our parental homes didn't always fit comfortably together. It has taken a while to understand this.

13. Reentry Children

Middle-aged parents of our generation are experiencing problems that have no precedent. Children have chosen from many models of authority figures in our diversified culture and in many instances this has caused great conflict in homes.

In *Adolescence* by Hans Sebald we find:

"American life shows frequent instance of friction and misunderstanding between the generations that are intense enough to resemble the encounter and clash between different cultures." [1]

Our children have grown up in the midst of one of the greatest scientific breakthroughs. Laymen parents are busy making a living and affording children an education. Regarding dad: "As a novelty in human history he is now instructed by his children."

The fact that parents cannot be competent in all areas can create a situation that makes children doubt their parents. Teenagers insist on being independent decision-makers in areas that in all time before were under parents' authority. Extrafamilial experts on television, in schools, on records are doing a considerable amount of instructing today while parents are still holding legal authority and affectional ties. Some children resent the authority. Parents are at great disadvantage to know how to cope with the situation. Sometimes it is possible for parents and children to sit together in the presence of a counselor or pastor and in dialogue come to understanding about their relationship. Because parents and children often bring so much feeling to the encounter, it takes a third person and sometimes a group situation to help maintain objectivity in dialogue.

There needs to be communication in families to determine where the boundaries of personalities begin and end. And where responsibilities begin and end. Mom's claim to power in "the guessing game" speaks to this. Relationships to space are boundaries that we can see and map out. As we observe the frequency of children wanting to reclaim childhood space in the home after a venture in the job market, an educational experience, we see need for a redefinition of spacial contract. A much harder contract to maintain is the relationship of feeling of the late adolescent teenager and middle-aged parent. How do parents and children respect each other as adults without continuing a mutual dependency relationship?

When do moms stop feeling responsible for their children's lives?

At what age do we refuse to be manipulated by guilt?

What money boundaries are set in as realistic control?

What responsibility do children assume for the upkeep and maintenance of the nest?

These are honest questions that I see middle-aged couples wrestling with.

In searching for an answer to the problem of dependency of adult children we remember the rootlessness of some life-styles which gave children no secondary relationship of permanent friends or relatives. There was absence of other supporting persons in extended family relationships such as grandparents. Children need stability. These factors are important. They complicate our consideration. But another important factor that must not be overlooked in modern homes is the fact that kids never had it so good! "Enlightened" psychology gave us rules to follow to produce superchildren. When things didn't go according to predictions, we blamed ourselves. We are finally having to cope with the fact that the children learned their psychology lessons right alongside the parents.

In talking to parents of adult children, I find a considerable amount of game-playing. Some parents "overlearned" parenting and feel so comfortable in that familiar relationship that they are unable to treat their children as adults. Children hook the weakness that moms and dads have to nurture and care for them and resettle into that safe secure harbor of home. We overreacted in our interpretation of "I love you just as you are," without making matching demands with guidelines for responsibility. Managing (manipulating) parents has become a studied art among kids. "You are the only parents who make these kinds of demands!" "Joe's dad is buying him a new C.B. radio, why can't I have one?" "Everybody I know stays out as late as they want to" serve as examples of studied effort to control parents.

Children become adults when they assume responsibility for themselves. Very often it is necessary for parents to get into some new patterns of relating to them to help bring this about.

When I have complained that I'm tired of housework, our children counter with: "Now, Mom, it's all in your point of view. Think of it as a hobby!"

Sometimes children from affluent homes do not have adequate tools for reality testing, because they take the basic ingredients of life for granted. Food, clothing, shelter, we realize are the essentials—when these needs are as automatically met as breathing along with all wants—the child is shifted over into an artificial set of values.

Searching for answers to our modern problems is a common bond, binding parents of all varieties together. We can get into a "blame game" or we can deal with life as an adventure. There are no detailed maps for pioneers.

SECTION V
THE
TIME
OF
YOUR
LIFE

14. Pine Sky

Ours has been an exciting and full life up to now. But Myron and I agree that we would not choose a rerun on any part of it. Speaking from the age of our fifties, we feel more relaxed about life and contented with each other than we have ever been. Other periods have had other feelings: pressured anxiety has given way to anticipated expectancy; excited passion to controlled response, frustrated busyness is paced to more limited commitment to others and deeper, broader commitment to each other and to life itself.

We are happy to assimilate our experience, relax in knowledge that major thrust is in the hands of another generation. Savor of life comes as when our granddaughter Sara, in a private moment said, "Mona, are you glad about me?"

We find refreshment in the miracle of nature that we knew as children. Several years ago we bought a cottage across the lake. We enjoy uninterrupted visits with each other, our children, grandchildren, and friends. Myron uses it for department picnics, evaluations, and parties.

This summer as we worked on this manuscript we took breaks to wade in the bayou, gather driftwood, and dig flowers for our natural flower beds. I want to mention my pot of pitcher plants—one of the few carnivorous (insect eating!) plants. They are found in the marsh here in our area.

Luscious blackberries that grow in wild abundance have provided dozens of cobblers for family and friends.

I remarked to Myron that it thrills me to see pine seed come spiraling from the hundred-foot pine tops to land on the lawn. My sense of economy protested nature's generosity with "yet they can't possibly have real purpose because we are going to keep this yard cut!" Myron gently reminded me, "The pine tree knows it will win. These trees were here before we were born."

I assessed my moment and deferred to the pine tree.

In the frame of reference of my "moment," I note a popular interest in death and dying. Myron's treatment of this subject is his book *Raise the Dead* in which he states that we need to evaluate taking life out of death, and death out of life. Our generation seems to be searching for meaning and feeling about this natural process. In our generation, death has become linked in a most unnatural way with violence and destruction. Projecting new unique ways of threatening and taking life by the cold impersonal television box is programmed entertainment. Traditionally, Americans have tried to hide death from the living. Our funerals are an example of this. Now we seem to need expert opinion to tell us how it really is. We want authority on how we should feel.

The life-styles of our generation have separated us from the family and community experience of watching death in natural family surroundings.

Recently our local newspapers carried two significant front-page stories: one was about longevity of life suggesting that perhaps there is a possibility that man can live to be eight hundred years old. The other story was written by Marjorie Roehl which she entitled, "At the Brink: perception between life and death." She dealt with persons' reactions to the near-death experience and quoted Myron as he told her of his own relationship with near-death persons.

"Many cases felt as though they were out of their bodies observing what went on around them. Some spoke of a 'personal escort,' others of being with people they loved. A number said they would no longer fear death."

The case I remember most clearly was a well-known clergyman who suffered a severe heart attack. Out of his body he could watch doctors working to bring him round. Then he was standing on a cliff from which he could see a beautiful land. He wanted to hurry to reach it and strongly resisted being dragged back.

"Perhaps," Myron suggested, "this was a dream state, and he did not wish to awaken to effort and pain. Of course, I can make no judgment."

He feels that a number of other patients experience something but did not want to discuss it for fear people would think them mentally ill as well as physically ill.

In discussing the article which promised an eight-hundred-year life, Myron and I agreed that we will decline to opt for that condition. We do not want to provide a home that takes care of fifty-year-old adolescents.

Middle age is a time to experience the moment. If habits and tradition from the past have served their purpose, declare freedom from them. Old tapes of "should" and "ought" need to be examined with the magnifying glass of present and future needs.

A sense of humor is one of the best ingredients to help relieve tension and anxiety. In middle age we have acquired the wisdom and experience to introduce another point of view. We have the knowledge and problem-solving skills from all of this living. Now is the most exciting time in the history of the world to be alive.

Claim your possibilities. Have a good life!

Notes

Introduction

1. Sam Keen, *Voices and Visions* (New York: Harper & Row, 1974), p. 189.

Chapter 1

1. Eric Berne, *What Do You Say After You Say Hello?* (New York: Bantam Books, 1973), p. 123.
2. Ibid., p. 131.
3. W. Hugh Missildine and Lawrence Galton, *Your Inner Conflicts* (New York: Simon & Schuster, 1975), p. 345.

Chapter 3

1. Thomas Traherne, *Centuries* (London: Faith Press, 1963), pp. 109-15.
2. Nathaniel Hawthorne, *The House of Seven Gables* (New York: Pocket Books, 1954), p. 147.
3. Op. cit., Berne, p. 31.
4. Ibid., p. 26.
5. Ernest Becker, *The Denial of Death* (New York: The Free Press, 1973), p. 37.
6. *Problems of the Middle Aged,* Comp. by Clyde B. Vedder. Article by Ruth Cavan (Springfield, Ill.: Charles C. Thomas, 1965), p. 86.
7. D. H. Lawrence, *Sons and Lovers* (New York: The Modern Library, 1962), p. 16.

8. Halbert L. Dunn, M.D., Ph.D., *High Level Wellness* (Arlington, Va.: R. W. Beatty, Ltd., 1967), p. 60.

9. From *Purity of Heart* (New York: Harper & Row), p. 27.

Chapter 4

1. Sam Keen, *Voices and Visions* (New York: First Perennial Library, 1976), p. 4.

2. This process is undertaken at length in a little book I wrote: *Raise the Dead* (Waco, Texas: Word, Inc., 1974).

Chapter 5

1. Fedor Dostoevski, *The Brothers Karamazov,* trans. by Constance Garnett (New York: Random House, Inc.), p. 820.

2. Raymond A. Moody, Jr., *Life After Life* (Atlanta: Mockingbird Books, 1975).

3. Karl A. Olsson, *Come to the Party* (Waco, Texas: Word, Inc., 1972), p. 11.

4. Soren Kierkegaard, *The Journals,* trans. by Alexander Dru (London: Oxford University Press, Amen House, 1959), p. 59.

5. Keen, *op. cit.,* p. 11.

Chapter 6

1. C. S. Lewis, *Grief Observed* (New York: Seabury Press, 1963).

Chapter 8

1. Fritz Perls, *The Gestalt Approach and Eye Witness to Therapy* (New York: Bantam Books, 1976), p. 33.

Chapter 11

1. Halbert L. Dunn, *High Level Wellness* (Arlington, Va.: R.

W. Beatty, Ltd.).

2. G. S. Serino, *Reducing After Forty* (Philadelphia: Auerbach Publishers, Inc.), 1971.

3. Joyce Brothers, *Better Than Ever* (New York: Simon & Schuster, 1975).

Chapter 13

1. Hans Sebald, *Adolescence: A Sociological Analysis* (New York: Appleton Century Crofts Education Division, Meredith Corporation).

ABOUT THE AUTHORS

Dr. Myron C. Madden is the director of the Department of Pastoral Care at the Southern Baptist Hospital, New Orleans, Louisiana. Mary Ben Madden is a free-lance writer, consultant, and teacher. They reside in New Orleans and have a second home across Lake Pontchartrain.

They often work together as a husband and wife team. Mary Ben serves as a consultant in the pastoral counseling center at New Orleans.

Mary Ben is a graduate of Louisiana State University. She has worked as a public schoolteacher in Virginia and Louisiana. Myron writes and speaks widely. His writing includes a monthly column in *Home Life* magazine. His previous books have been *The Power to Bless* and *Raise the Dead.*

They have five children: Myron, Jr., Julia Ann, John Benjamin, and Merritt. Myron likes "fishin' and piddlin' "—Mary Ben plays the piano, sews, reads, and "parents children."